JIMI HENDRIX

JOHN FARALACO

with

KEN VOSS

Director, Jimi Hendrix Information Management Institute

LONGMEADOW
PRESS

This 1993 edition published by
Longmeadow Press
201 High Ridge Road
Stamford CT 06904

Produced by
Brompton Books Corporation
15 Sherwood Place
Greenwich CT 06830

ISBN 0-681-41873-7

Printed in Hong Kong

0 9 8 7 6 5 4 3 2 1

The discographies and tour itineraries are copy-
right © Jimi Hendrix Information Management
Institute and reproduced by expressed permission.

ACKNOWLEDGMENTS
We wish to thank Mr Ken Voss of JIMI—the Jimi
Hendrix Information Management Institute of Des
Plaines, Illinois—who provided many hours
of valuable research time, and opened the
JIMI archives for our use.

**Designed and captioned by
Bill Yenne and Tom Debolski**

PHOTO CREDITS
AGS Archives: 13 (top), 17, 19, 21 (right), 41
    (right), 44 (bottom), 49 (bottom)
Brompton Photo Library: 60 (both)
© Mike Charity/Globe Photos: 13 (bottom)
Collection of the author: 7, 11, 12, 14, 16, 21 (left),
    26 (both), 30-31 (left), 34, 40, 41 (left), 43
    (both), 45 (top), 47, 52, 57 (both), 61, 62, 68,
    71 (all), 74 (both)
© Tony Gale/Pictorial Press: 8, 32
© Globe Photos: 23 (top)
Property of the Jimi Hendrix Information
    Management Institute, all rights reserved, used
    by permission: 2, 23 (bottom), 24-25 (both),
    29 (bottom), 38, 39, 42, 44 (top), 53 (top), 54,
    56, 58 (both)
© Allan Koss, all rights reserved, used by
    permission: 6, 9, 10, 46, 48, 50-51, 64
© Pictorial Press: 18 (both), 20, 22, 27, 28
    (both), 29 (top), 33, 34 (top), 35, 36 (bottom),
    37, 45 (bottom), 59, 66, 67 (both), 70, 75
© Ted Russell/Globe Photos: 49 (top)
© UPI/Bettmann: 53 (bottom)
© 1993 Bill Yenne: 1, 4-5, 15 (both), 31 (right),
    36 (top), 63

CONTENTS

PROLOGUE

What has been, will be,
'Tis the under-law of life:
'Tis the song of sky and sea,
To the key of calm and strife.

Above: **Jimi Hendrix in a rare, quiet backstage moment at the peak of his career.**

Facing page: **Hendrix and his Band of Gypsys on stage at the Woodstock festival on 18 August 1969. It was the culmination of the sixties, and the beginning of the end of an era.**

He was probably the greatest rock guitarist of his era, and perhaps of all time. There were other rockers, certainly, who were equally notable, but Jimi Hendrix holds a special place in that pantheon. He was a prophet, and he was endowed with an awesome splendor, burning with wild radiance, the enlightener of daily life in the sixties. He was unique.

In looking back over the quarter century since Jimi's time, we have repeatedly endeavored to explain that the heroes of the sixties are intrinsically of the same material, having been given a great soul, open to the divine significance of life, given to speak of this, to sing of this, to work for this, in a great, enduring manner. These were the heroes upon whom the outward shape of the time and the environment depended. Jimi Hendrix was a kind of prophet. In him we recall a light of inspiration.

He united us with the unseen, that spiritual oneness that we sought in those days. Hendrix was a spiritual captain of the people. He guided us through his work, and even today the ideal of him is that he was what we can call a voice from the unseen rock & roll heaven, interpreting a more familiar manner, unfolding the same to the people. It is the unseen heaven—the 'open secret of the universe.'

The decade of the sixties was a turbulent epoch, full of anger, confusion and danger, and the spiritual captains who led us through that became, especially to us who lived in those times, more notable than any others. They led the people, not to quiet, faithful music as in smooth times, but to a sort of

PROLOGUE

Right: Jimi enjoying a cigarette backstage at the Saville Theatre, London, January 1967.

Facing page: Hendrix at Woodstock in 1969 is the very image of the intensity that best defines his painfully brief career.

spiritual conflict, in those dismembered times. These men and women were prophets inasmuch as they were our best performers. One may ask, is not every true performer, by nature, a spiritual being first of all? Yes, but those times were different, and so were the people by whom we remember the essence of those times. The Beatles. Bob Dylan. The Stones. The Who. The Airplane. Janis Joplin. Jimi Hendrix.

Each generation finds that something credible to his grandfather is incredible to him, false to him, inconsistent with something he has discovered or observed. This is the inevitable history of every generation, and in the history of people, we see it summed up into great revolutions, new epochs. The people of the sixties found no such thing extant as the Beatles' Strawberry Fields or Hendrix's Electric Ladyland. It is not there, so we ceased to believe it to be there. So it is with all beliefs whatsoever in this world—all systems of belief, and systems of practice that spring from these.

Two hundred years ago, it was written that all generations were thought of as 'lost' and 'wrong,' and only that this little section of the present generation might be saved and right. Yet all marched forward, like all generations since the beginning.

Every one of us, as we now know, is not only a learner but a doer. We learn with the mind given us, but with the same mind we discover, invent and devise something of our own. Without originality there is no life or spirit. No man whatever believes, or can believe, exactly what his grandfather believed. He enlarges somewhat, by fresh discovery, his view of the universe, and consequently his idea of the universe—which is an infinite universe, and can never be embraced wholly or finally by any view in any conceivable enlargement.

The great rockers of the sixties, in various situations, exemplified heroic forms of human existence in their work, such as

the theories of life worthy to be sung by Bob Dylan or the practices of life sung by John Lennon. It is worth noting that in this time period song writers were able to make a spiritual representation, which took in the whole universe and was completely satisfactory in all its parts. This is certainly represented by the highly acute intellect of Dylan—one of the greatest in the world. In the course of another decade, it became debatable to common intellects, became deniable, and is now, to every one of us, flatly incredible, as obsolete as the Perry Como fifties.

It was a more perilous venue, and a most memorable one. Like the others, Hendrix appealed, and still appeals, to heaven's invisible justice against Earth's visible force. He knew that it—the invisible—is strong and alone. He was a believer in the truth of things, a seer seeing through the show of things. If he had not first been a prophet, he would never have been much good as a performer.

The prophet is a person that cannot fail. The performer indeed is the product and ultimate agent of performance or prophecy, with its fierceness. There would have been no wild Rolling Stones and Who, had there been no early Dylan. Rough practical endeavor, from San Francisco to London, from New York to Hollywood, enabled Jimi Hendrix to speak. The poet is a symptom like his epoch itself, and he has reached perfection and is finished. Before long, there will be a new epoch and new performers are needed. We now see the reverse process, which also may be necessary, and which also may be carried on in the heroic manner.

It is curious how this should be necessary, yet it *is* necessary. The mild shining of the poet's light has to give way to the fierce lightning of the performer. In Jimi Hendrix, *both* manifested themselves profoundly.

THE VOODOO CHILD

For fate is master here,
   He laughs at human wiles;
He scepters every fear
   And fetters any smiles.

Jimi Hendrix was born in Seattle, Washington at 10:15 am on 27 November 1942. Lucille Jeter Hendrix named her son Johnny Allen Hendrix. Born there, was a mighty man, whose light was to flame as the beacon over long decades and epochs. The world of music and its history was waiting for this man.

Lucille was severely underweight and barely 18 years old when her first son was born, and the experience of giving birth took a terrible toll on her physically. On top of this, she had contracted tuberculosis. Her husband, Al, was in the Army in Alabama at the time and couldn't get a furlough to come home to see his son. When he demanded a furlough, he was thrown into the stockade until it was time for his unit to go overseas.

When Al Hendrix returned from World War II in 1945, he discovered that Lucille had sent their little son—now nearly three years old—to live with her relatives in Berkeley, California, so he left Seattle to go south in search of the son he'd never met.

When he finally did find his boy, Lucille's relatives insisted that he should just go away and let them keep the boy because Johnny knew them better. What could a father do? Al simply wouldn't stand for it, and told them so. He took his son back with him to Seattle, where he rented an apartment at 124 Tenth Avenue and set about changing his son's name. On 11 September 1946, Al Hendrix renamed Johnny Allen Hendrix for his father's long-deceased older brother, named James Marshall Hendrix.

Above: **Hendrix checking out the sound system prior to the Monterey International Pop Festival, June 1967.**

Facing page: **A contemplative Jimi.**

THE VOODOO CHILD

Right: A very young Jimi Hendrix, fresh from Seattle and ready to rock & roll.

Opposite top: The legendary Fats Domino was an inspiration to Jimi Hendrix and the other young black performers who came of age in the sixties.

Opposite bottom: Off-stage Jimi was a soft-spoken, gentle person. On-stage he exploded with stunning musical fury.

Hardship, a rigorous necessity, was the boy's companion. No man, nor any thing, would put on a false face to flatter Jimi Hendrix. He had to grow among things, not among the show of things. A boy of rude figure, yet with his large soul, full of all faculty and sensibility, it was this task to get acquainted with *realities*, and keep acquainted with them, at whatever cost. Jimi struggled up through boyhood, better and worse, displaying, in spite of all hindrances, the most fabulous musical ability. He was a youth nursed in whirlwinds, in desolate darkness and difficulty. He was destined to step forth at last from the Northwest, strong and true.

Meanwhile, Lucille moved in with the husband she'd never really gotten to know before he was drafted, and their second son, Leon Hendrix, was born in 1948. They lived together off and on until 1950, when they finally divorced.

Al and Lucille were living in a housing project on Yesler Way when Lucille decided to leave her husband and their children. Al tried to manage as a single parent, but found it too difficult.

At last he sent the boys to live with his sister in Vancouver, British Columbia. When her husband died in 1952, she sent the boys back to Seattle, where Al had a job working for the Boeing Airplane Company, and soon after their arrival, he enrolled Leon and James at Leschi Elementary School in Seattle's Central District.

Al bought James his first acoustic guitar—actually nothing more than a ukulele—for five dollars. When he quickly outgrew it, Al found him an electric one. James soon discovered he had quite a talent for the instrument, and would spend countless hours exploring its joys and its magic. Both of his parents had always been fond of music—especially big band dance music—and it was gratifying for his dad to see James taking such an interest.

By the time James was in his teens—they were calling him Jimi now—the barrier of segregation in the popular music industry had begun to disappear. Only a decade before, black artists recorded 'race records' solely for black record labels and played only in black clubs. At that time, white dance bands with black musicians present were practically unheard of, and mainstream radio did not play 'race' music. By the mid-fifties, however, things began to rapidly change. Black groups, such as the Orioles, the Moonglows and the Drifters, were making the transition over the color line, and soon crossover hits were no longer the exception to the long-standing rule. Rock & roll was born, midwived equally by white artists, such as Elvis Presley, Carl Perkins and Bill Haley as by black artists, such as Chuck Berry, Fats Domino and Little Richard. Southern white hillbilly music had merged with southern black blues to create a phenomenon that would alter the course of musical history, not only in America but around the world.

Rock & roll inspired Jimi Hendrix, as it did all those who would carry the baton into immortality in the sixties. He was 18 when he joined Fred Rollins' band, the Rocking Kings, in 1960, and he soon was rated as one of the best guitar players in the Northwest. The Kings played Seattle and did quite well in Vancouver, but broke up when Fred Rollins was drafted by the United States Army. Jimi never finished his last year at Garfield High School. He was impressed by Rollins' uniform and decided that he wanted to be a paratrooper.

Hendrix entered the Army in 1960 and joined the 101st Airborne Division, the notorious 'Screaming Eagles,' so named for their insignia. He enjoyed the almost ethereal experience of parachuting from airplanes and the silent solitude of being alone in the sky, but he discovered that his first love—his guitar—was the essence of his life.

Soon he was playing at clubs around the 101st Airborne's headquarters at Fort Campbell, Kentucky and traveling around

This page: It was while he was attending James A Garfield High School in Seattle *(below)* in the late 1950s that a young Jimi Hendrix joined his first band, The Rocking Kings.

In February 1968, he returned to Seattle a global superstar and stopped by Garfield to pick up an honorary diploma. A bust of Jimi *(right)* in the high school's library commemorates the event.

Facing page: A soulful Jimi lets his guitar do the talking.

Above: Jimi Hendrix joined Curtis Knight *(center)* and his band in December 1965. His membership in Knight's band was short-lived, but Hendrix played sessions with Knight as late as 1967. A large body of recorded work still survives from this collaboration *(see page 72).*

the South on his weekend furloughs, listening to Southern blues at the source. When he was discharged from the Army, Hendrix stayed in the South, playing music with Billy Cox and Johnny Snead. In 1963, he joined Little Richard Penniman's band. By the early sixties, however, Little Richard's career was in decline and the money that had flowed a decade earlier had dried up, leaving him a mere pittance to pay his sidemen. Hendrix left the band to join Ike Turner's Blues Band, and he also played with legendary blues guitarists like Albert King.

By the spring of 1964, Hendrix had made his way to New York, where he met Ronnie Isley of the Isley Brothers, who hired him for the band's North American tour. At the end of the year, Hendrix left the Isley Brothers for Curtis Knight's band, the Squires, with whom he would record some of his earliest sides. Also with Knight, Jimi played numerous club dates in the New York-New Jersey area.

When he first moved to New York City, Hendrix lived in Harlem, but eventually he was spending much of this time at the jazz, folk and rhythm & blues clubs in Greenwich Village and on the East Side. Here he met Bob Dylan and played with Joey

Dee, the king of the Twist craze. Jimi's influences were as eclectic as the great city itself.

One recalls that episode in the legends of the Mahabharata where Satyavan set out, ax in hand—an ax is a metaphor for an electric guitar—through the wilderness. The morning was wondrously bright. Gigantic climbers grew in the thickets in great profusion, interlacing the smaller trees. The sunlight lay upon the surface and birds hovered above or settled down amidst the lotus near the water's edge. Away in the distance, the Himalayas lifted their snowy brows into the blue heavens and reflected the sun's rays from their icy peaks. For Jimi, ax in hand in the wilderness, the peaks were indeed distant, but he would surmount them.

By the end of 1965, Hendrix had formed his own band— Jimmy James and the Blue Flames—and had landed a more or less regular gig at the Cafe Wha? in Greenwich Village. It was here that he was encountered by John Hammond, Jr, the son of John Hammond, the legendary blues and folk producer for Columbia Records—the man who had 'discovered' Bob Dylan. The younger Hammond, a self-styled producer/promo-

Above: Chas Chandler formed the Jimi Hendrix Experience in England in October 1966, with Jimi on guitar and vocals, Mitch Mitchell *(left)* on drums and Noel Redding *(right)* on bass.

They had their official debut on 21 December, but they'd already been together for two months. It was with this band that Hendrix recorded almost all of the studio tracks released during his lifetime.

Left: The Jimi Hendrix Experience during one of the several television appearances they made in 1967.

ter, got Hendrix a booking at the Cafe Au Go Go, then the most upscale club in Greenwich Village. This in turn led to Jimi meeting members of the Rolling Stones and the Animals, who were—aside from the Beatles—the hottest English rock bands in the world in 1965. Linda Keith, the girlfriend of Stones' lead guitarist Keith Richard, took more than a passing interest in the wild guitarist from Seattle and introduced him to Chas Chandler, who decided that Hendrix would be a sensation in England.

Unfolding now were the great talents and virtues implanted in him. It was inevitable that he should rise to importance, and eventually stardom, in the world. It was in his twenty-third year that Jimi Hendrix first saw London.

The succession of events that began with Jimi's arrival in New York had culminated in a pivotal career move. In New York he'd had a small following. He had established a subsistence career and, had he stayed there, he probably could have eked out a living and a place as a footnote in the history of rock, but in England he was destined to step over the threshold of immortality. Chas Chandler first introduced Jimi Hendrix to England on 21 September 1966. Thanks to Chandler's promotional efforts, his reputation had preceded him, but Jimi was easily able to live up to the hype.

Chandler also helped Hendrix audition a back-up band, which would be selected from among the musicians who queued up to try out for work with the Animals, whom Chandler had also managed until just prior to meeting Jimi. They decided to select only two musicians, and picked Noel Redding to play bass and Mitch Mitchell for drums. At that time, the idea of a three-instrument group was innovative. Usually bands consisted of a bass, drums and two guitars— rhythm and lead—so a three instrument group was seen as representing an attempt to eliminate the distinction between background and foreground. Another such three-man group, born at the same time and also destined for greatness, was Cream, which had Jack Bruce on bass, Ginger Baker on drums and the great Eric Clapton on guitar.

Redding, Mitchell, Hendrix and his manager created their new band—the Jimi Hendrix Experience—on 12 October 1966.

Jimi had been in England less than a month when Chandler started to book the band into the best clubs in London. Johnny Hallyday, the French rock star, saw the band at one of their first gigs and flew them to Paris for a huge show he was staging at the Olympia on 18 October. Within weeks, the Jimi Hendrix Experience was making television appearances and cropping up everywhere in the London press. The strange black man from America, who no one had heard of a month

Above: The British supergroup Cream, a contemporary of the Jimi Hendrix Experience, included *(left to right)* Ginger Baker on drums, Eric Clapton on guitar and Jack Bruce on bass.

before, was suddenly the talk of the town—and everyone was talking—from the night club society crowd to the musicians who were Jimi's direct competitors—Pete Townshend of the Who, members of the Stones, Eric Clapton and even the Beatles. Jimi Hendrix was meeting the men who were shaping the history of music in the 1960s—and the women who inspired them. He met and formed a close relationship with Marianne Faithful, a pop star of minor reputation who was best known in 1966 as Mick Jagger's girlfriend.

While all of this activity was under way, Chas Chandler was pressing for a record deal, and the Jimi Hendrix Experience went into the studio to record what Chandler hoped he could market as their first single. They recorded *Hey Joe*, a staple from Jimi's live shows, backed with *Stone Free*, one of Jimi's own compositions. Chandler first took the tape to Decca, one of the largest labels in England, which was famous for eagerly

Above: Jimi's friend Marianne Faithful, the sultry queen of London's rock scene in 1966-67. She was Mick Jagger's significant other and enjoyed a moment in the sun before her career collapsed under the weight of drugs.

Left: A promotional photo of the Jimi Hendrix Experience circa late 1967.

Opposite: Jimi in London, January 1967.

signing the Rolling Stones after having turned down the Beatles in 1962. Perhaps it was a good omen that Jimi Hendrix was to suffer the same fate as the Beatles.

With moral support from Kit Lambert, the Who's manager, Chandler was not discouraged and kept shopping the tape to other labels. Finally, he struck a deal with Track, and *Hey Joe* was released on 16 December 1966, in time for the Christmas rush. The single did moderately well, entering the charts at number 48. The Jimi Hendrix Experience continued its relentless round of club dates, yet the stardom of which they dreamed remained elusive.

Jimi's world—his London world that winter—included the pantheon of English rock: Mick Jagger, Eric Clapton, Pete Townshend, John Mayall and Marianne Faithful. He hung out with Chas Chandler and became friends with Brian Jones, the ill-fated guitarist who everyone now remembers as the soul of

Above: Like many young bands starting out in show business, the Experience toured England as part of a British Pop Package Tour in early 1967. This photo shows Jimi backstage with tourmates *(left to right)* Cat Stevens, Gary Leeds and Engelbert Humperdinck.

the Rolling Stones. Coincidentally, Jones was also to die tragically in 1969, just a year before Jimi's own spirit was unplugged from the amp of life.

Jimi met girls . . . Kathy Etchingham . . . Chrissie Charles . . . and drifted in and out of relationships. He spent his days in bed, sometimes alone, sometimes not. He spent his nights in clubs, on stage or cruising with Brian Jones. They took LSD and visited a place that neither realized had existed before.

It was during that dark, London winter of smoggy, purple twilights that he wrote *Purple Haze*, the song by which he would best be remembered, the song in which he penned these immortal lines:

'Purple haze all in my brain. Lately things just don't seem the same. Acting funny but I don't know why, 'scuse me while I kiss the sky. Purple haze all around, don't know if I'm comin' up or down. Am I happy or in misery? Whatever it is, that girl put a spell on me. Purple haze all in my eyes, don't know if it's day or night. You got me going, blowing my mind. Is it tomorrow or just the end of time?'

When *Purple Haze* hit the charts, it rocketed skyward and Jimi was suddenly on people's minds. Not all of their thoughts were good. Some newspapers dubbed his prose 'drug lyrics,' and Jimi became a controversial demon of the then-emerging counterculture.

On 29 January 1967, the long-awaited turning point came with a double bill at the Saville Theater featuring the Experience with the Who. Everyone who was anybody in the hot London rock scene was present, and the concert was, predictably, a sensation. Within a week, *Hey Joe* had reached number four on the charts. The Jimi Hendrix Experience had finally arrived.

Inspired by success and accolades from his peers, Jimi began to record some of the songs by which he would later best be remembered, including *Purple Haze*, the allegory of life in the gloom of London's winter, and *The Stars That Play with Laughing Sam's Dice* (STP/LSD), whose title was a reference to psychedelic mind expansion that preceded John Lennon's later hit *Lucy in the Sky with Diamonds* (LSD). However, it was the cover tunes, like *Hey Joe* and the Troggs' *Wild Thing*, that best showcased Jimi's power and frenzy in performance. It was about this time that he discovered, accidentally, that an electric guitar made bizarre sounds when it was being smashed to bits on stage. He also discovered that his audiences loved it, so this practice became a staple of his live act. On 31 March 1967, he opened for the Walker Brothers at Finsbury Park. He began his show with *Purple Haze* and the audience went crazy. He closed with his new song called *Fire*, in which he intoned, 'I have only one burning desire, let me stand next to your fire!'

To underscore the song, he doused his Fender Stratocaster with lighter fluid and lit it with a match. The instant inferno frightened everyone on stage and in the audience. It was as though Hendrix had gone insane in an orgy of self-immolation. It was reminiscent of the mythology of the Vedas, where the gods Indra and Soma—the guardians of Brahmans—burn the devils. They destroy them, throw them down, or, as the story goes, they 'hew down the madmen, suffocate them, kill them; hurl them away, and slay the voracious. Indra and Soma, up together against the cursing demon! May he burn and hiss like an oblation in the fire! Put your everlasting hatred upon the villain who hates the Brahman, who eats flesh, and whose look is abominable. Indra and Soma hurl the evil-doer into the pit, even into unfathomable darkness! May your strength be full of wrath to hold out that no one may come out again.'

When Jimi Hendrix stepped from the inferno that night, the audience thundered its approval, and the stage manager threatened to file a lawsuit. How do you sue Indra? How do you sue the ethereal?

Overnight, Jimi Hendrix had become England's number one outlaw and number one sex symbol. All that remained, was for him to relaunch his career in America. With *Purple Haze* now in the number one spot on British charts, this was suddenly

Above: While living in England, Hendrix made many friends who were involved in the rock music scene, including members of the Rolling Stones. He became particularly close with Brian Jones *(bottom right).*

Below: Jimi with girlfriend Kathy Etchingham in London during the winter of 1967.

These pages: Jimi Hendrix plays a private party? Yes, in Belgium on 4 March 1967, he played the D'Assas Law Society Graduation Ball at the *Faculté de Droit*.

The sixties had literally *exploded* volcanically, and there would be long troubled periods before we could look back rationally. We find Hendrix to have been a breaker of idols, no less than any other prophet. The wooden gods of fifties' pop were not more hateful to the Rolling Stones than the sixties' pop scene was to Hendrix. 'You'll never hear surf music again,' he sang.

Above: Jimi Hendrix on guitar during a 1967 concert appearance.

Above right: The cover for the British version of the Jimi Hendrix Experience's first album *Are You Experienced*. It was released in May 1967 and immediately became an essential element of popular culture on both sides of the Atlantic.

easier than he could have dreamed even six months before. On 20 May 1967, the Jimi Hendrix Experience signed with Reprise Records in the United States and pocketed a check for $120,000.

The first Jimi Hendrix Experience album was *Are You Experienced*. It is still considered by many as one of the dozen classic albums from the sixties. The album was virtually dripping with memorable hits. *Hey Joe* and *Purple Haze* were there, and so were *Fire*, *Foxy Lady* and *Manic Depression*. In the United States, the album caught the public by surprise, but in England it *entered* the charts at number *three*.

Even though most people still remember Woodstock as the definitive sixties rock festival, in fact it was more of a sixties retrospective than a vibrant spark of brilliance or transcendent magic. It was powerful. It was moving. But it was not original.

Originality was born on the other coast. Originality went back to the acid tests of late 1965 and evolved surreptitiously through the scene at the Fillmore and the Avalon Ballroom in San Francisco in 1966 before it exploded in crystal clarity in Golden Gate Park on 14 January 1967. A new epoch in human history was born that day. The counterculture had moved from being an ambiguous idea shared by a handful of disconnected souls to a movement—a movement that would shake the foundations of mainstream culture.

All through the ages, the so-called supernatural—the intrusion of the spiritual realm into that of the material—has been a matter of belief. Religions of all lands are saturated with the miraculous and the preternatural. With the advent of modern science, much of the superstition and folly connected with matters of this kind vanished. The universal reign of law being

Above: **A candid shot of Mitch, Jimi and Noel enjoying a quiet moment behind the scenes.**

established, of necessity the miraculous and the supernatural, as commonly understood, ceased to exist. But with the establishment of the law of evolution in matter and mind, there then evolved a new phase of what had been considered supernatural in the sense of its being beyond, and above, the temporal.

Musicians like Bob Dylan and the Beatles—who embodied this ideal of the miraculous in the daily life of the sixties— were embraced by the counterculture, but they were not part of it. At first the pop music community was taken aback by a culture even farther from the mainstream than they were, but soon the two would come together in the event still recalled as the first rock festival, the progenitor of them all.

In the realm of light that was the sixties, there were those who labored as teachers among the restless masses. They were not at first seen as human beings, but only as patches of light that blinded and dazzled the undeveloped spirits. But as they continued to magnetize their subjects, the latter gradually began to feel a quickening force—the quickening force from

the magnetic light and breath, the never-failing, penetrating power of the stimulating force within—and even the most hardened entity was reached and vitalized.

In the sphere of light there were many masters who could gather a substance from the vapor, which they hardened to any degree at will: formed, beautiful and fragrant from the atmosphere, by the spirit chemist, who breathes upon it and gives it life and magic.

The Monterey International Pop Festival was held over three days and nights between 16 and 18 June 1967. Monterey Pop would be headlined by the Mamas & the Papas. The Who would be there, as would a new group called Buffalo Springfield. The Beatles were invited but declined to appear. (They had played their last show a year before and would never play together in public as a group again.) However, their erstwhile publicist, Derek Taylor, was hired to do publicity, and he introduced John Phillips of the Mamas & the Papas to Paul McCartney, who suggested a hit new band that was exploding like an atom bomb in England and firing the imaginations of all who saw them—The Jimi Hendrix Experience.

Monterey Pop was also a showcase for another singer— then virtually unknown—who would emerge from the Festival a superstar, and who ironically, would be found dead within a week of Jimi three years later: Janis Joplin.

Above: The boys waiting to take the stage during a tour of England.

Right: Jimi's performance stunned the audience at the Monterey Pop Festival. It was America's first exposure to the Experience in concert.

Opposite above: Hendrix and the Experience performing at the Roundhouse, London in late 1967.

Opposite below: Mama Cass shares a secret with Jimi backstage at the Saville Theatre, London.

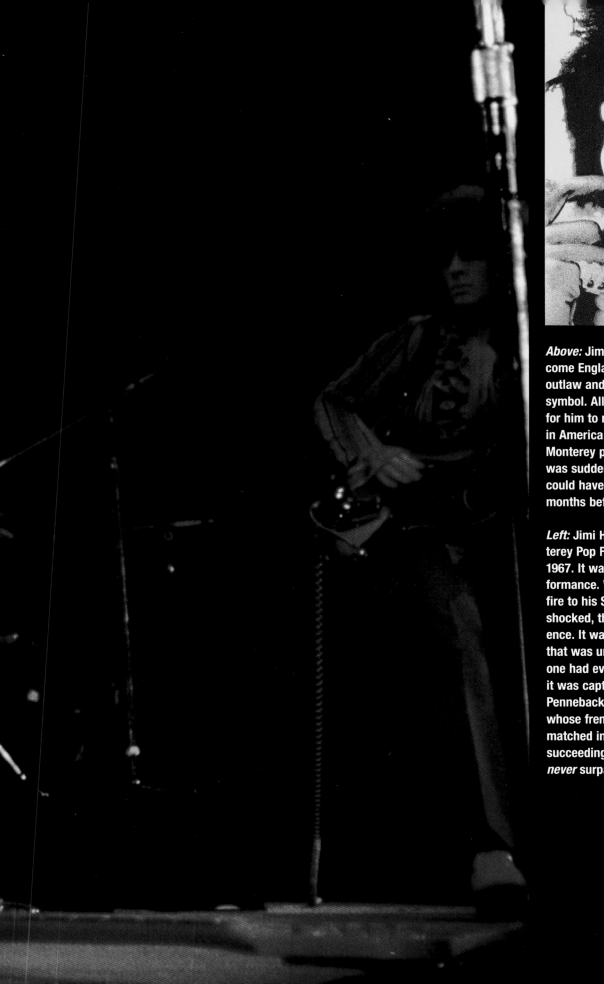

Above: Jimi Hendrix had become England's number one outlaw and number one sex symbol. All that remained was for him to relaunch his career in America. After his explosive Monterey performance, this was suddenly easier than he could have dreamed even six months before.

Left: Jimi Hendrix at the Monterey Pop Festival on 18 June 1967. It was a legendary performance. When Hendrix set fire to his Stratocaster, it shocked, then thrilled the audience. It was a performance that was unlike anything anyone had ever seen. Fortunately, it was captured on film by DA Pennebacker, for it was a show whose frenzy has been matched in intensity over the succeeding three decades, but *never* surpassed.

Above: A playful Jimi Hendrix poses with his guitar backstage in London, 1967.

Facing page: Jimi and the boys hanging out at the London flat that Hendrix shared with the group's manager Chas Chandler, May 1967.

Backed by Big Brother & the Holding Company, Janis stunned the audience. But *nobody* was ready for Jimi. He opened his set with *Hey Joe* and slid into Dylan's *Like a Rolling Stone.* He closed with *Wild Thing* and a performance that was unlike anything anyone had ever seen. Fortunately, it was captured on film by DA Pennebacker, for it was a show whose frenzy has been matched in intensity over the succeeding three decades, but *never* surpassed.

No one in the United States had ever seen a man set fire to a guitar on stage before, but that was how Jimi ended *Wild Thing.* The guitar—still plugged into an amp—howled uncontrollably as it was consumed by fire. The audience—still plugged into the Hendrix phenomenon—howled uncontrollably as it was consumed by the spectacle before them. And their howling went on for a half hour after he left the stage. The Grateful Dead were supposed to go on next, but how could they?

The scene was the hottest thing in the history of pop music. The whole world was looking on. It was the shout of the awakening of a generation.

When Jimi Hendrix arrived in Los Angeles 48 hours later, he found that his reputation had preceded him. The phrase 'overnight sensation' was an understatement. Everyone on the LA music scene begged for an audience. *Purple Haze* was on the radio.

Offers of gigs and tours were offered everywhere he went—as he drifted from crash pad to crash pad to million dollar homes in the Hollywood Hills that were complete with expensive cars, swimming pools, bathing beauties and open invitations.

The Jimi Hendrix Experience started to get booked into large arenas, but incredibly, they were booked to open for the Monkees, a band that had been contrived artificially to star in a television situation comedy loosely based on the Beatles' movie *A Hard Day's Night* (1964). The idea that Jimi Hendrix—an innovator on the leading edge of the counterculture—would be booked as an opening act for such a group, whose appeal was to pre-teens, was incongruous, preposterous and even surreal. But it happened.

Hendrix had stayed at the home of the Monkees' Peter Tork when he was in Los Angeles, and they had apparently gotten along well enough, but they really didn't realize what they were about to do. As could be expected, the match between the two groups didn't work, and Jimi left the Monkees tour and was booked into more appropriate venues, such as Bill Graham's Fillmore Auditorium in San Francisco on 20 to 25 June 1967, his debut in the city that had defined the counterculture.

Hendrix on-stage *(facing page)* and off *(above)* in the last weeks of 1967.

Below: Hendrix shares a relaxed moment with Scottish folk singer Donovan Leitch. Donovan's career was peaking at the time Jimi's was taking off.

The summer of 1967—the so-called Summer of Love— was a time of magic moments when the spiritual and ethereal seemed so close. The higher spiritual essences of the material planet gravitate to form a spiritual world. So in turn do higher emanations from this spiritual world, its refined essence gravitates to an appropriate plane of action superior to that occupied by the world from which they sprang, and these help to form a second spirit-world, the third sphere as it is called. But not from the sublimated emanations alone, from one primary spirit-world or second sphere, are formed the third spheres of immensity. 'Purple haze all in my brain. Lately things just don't seem the same. Acting funny but I don't know why, 'scuse me while I kiss the sky.'

The law of universal unity and fraternity—seen on the streets of San Francisco that summer—became exemplified in larger measure in the process of development of each successive series of spirit-worlds. 'Purple haze all around, don't know if I'm comin' up or down. Am I happy or in misery? Whatever it is, that girl put a spell on me.'

At the end of the summer, Hendrix returned to Europe for dates in London and across the continent through the first of 1968, with a grand finale in Paris on 29 January 1968.

The sixties had literally *exploded* volcanically, and there would be long troubled periods before we could look back rationally. We find Hendrix to have been a breaker of idols, no less than any other prophet. The wooden gods of the fifties' pop music scene were not more hateful to the Rolling Stones than sixties' pop was to Hendrix.

It is the property of every hero, in every time, in every place and situation, that he come back to reality; that he stand upon things and not shows of things—the first stroke of honest demolition of an ancient thing grown false and idolatrous.

One often hears it said that the sixties introduced a new era, radically different from any the world had ever seen before. By this revolt against the rigid status quo of the Eisenhower era, everyone became his or her own person and learned, among other things, that we must never trust any spiritual hero-captain anymore. Sixties rock was the grand root from which our whole subsequent musical history branches out, for the spiritual will always body itself forth in the temporal history of music. The spiritual is the beginning of the temporal.

Whole ages, like the sixties, are original. All people in them, or most of them, sense this. These are the great and fruitful ages for music: every musician in all spheres is at work not on semblance but on substance. Nearly every song and nearly every album issued is a result. The general sum of such work is great; for all of it is genuine and it tends toward one goal.

THE VOODOO CHILD

On 24 February 1968, the Jimi Hendrix Experience released their second album: *Axis: Bold as Love*. The cover paid tribute to the Hindu deity Brahma, and the lyrics recalled the characteristics of his various manifestations.

According to Hindu doctrine, Brahma had abandoned the form he had used, and the form thus abandoned became night. Then from his *mouth* proceeded gods, and the form which he then abandoned became day, for goodness predominated in it. He next adopted another form, and the progenitors were born from his side, and the body which he then abandoned became the evening twilight. Brahma then assumed another body, and from this, men were born, and the body thus abandoned became the morning twilight.

Thus gods, men, demons and progenitors were reconstructed from previous forms, and the bodies which Brahma abandoned became day, night, dawn and evening. Afterward, the hairs of Brahma, which were shriveled up, fell from his head and became cobras. The creator of the world, being incensed by the loss of his hair, created fierce beings who were denominated goblins. They were malignant fiends and eaters of flesh.

'Purple haze all in my brain. Lately things just don't seem the same. Acting funny but I don't know why, 'scuse me while I kiss the sky.'

In the form of Siva, Brahma was said to be living in the Himalaya Mountains, together with his wife Parvati, the daughter of the mountain. She was worshipped in Bengal under the name of Durga.

'Purple haze all around, don't know if I'm comin' up or down. Am I happy or in misery? Whatever it is, that girl put a spell on me.'

The name Siva means 'auspicious.' He is a good allegory for Jimi Hendrix. Like the other deities, he is represented as the Supreme God, while having over a thousand names, such as The Lord of the Universe, The Destroyer, The Reproducer, and The Conqueror of Life and Death. His worshipers are called Saivas, who exalt him to the highest place in the heavens. He is represented as Time, Justice, Fire, Water, the Sun and also as the Creator and the Destroyer. His personal appearance must be rather striking, as his throat is dark blue and his hair light red, thickly matted together on the top of his head. He has five faces, in one of which is a third eye situated in the center of the forehead, and pointing up and down.

As Hendrix wrote, 'He smiles—towering in shiny metallic purple armor, Queen Jealousy ... waits behind him ... blue are the life-giving waters ... they quietly understand: Once happy turquoise armies lay opposite, ready, but wonder why the fight is on, but they're all bold as love. Just ask the Axis.'

Above: Mitch, Noel and Jimi sporting the colorful fashions popular during the Summer of Love.

Opposite above: A 1968 poster showing Jimi Hendrix in psychedelic splendor.

Opposite below: In the dressing room at the Saville Theatre, London. Jimi, like all touring performers, killed many an hour in rooms such as this waiting for his moment in the limelight.

ARE YOU EXPERIENCED?

And sometimes we may think
This cannot—will not—be:
Some waves must rise, some sink,
Out on the midnight sea.

For Jimi Hendrix, the formative years were over by 1968. He was on the threshold of a turning point in his life. Soon he would change, but still he was the introspective, glimmering genius, at one with the inner structure of nature. The soul of all his voices and utterances was inherent in his perfect music. Poetry can be called *musical thought*. It is a man's sincerity and depth of vision that make him a poet, and the poet is he who *thinks* in music. At bottom, it still turns on the power of intellect. See deep enough and you see musically, the heart of nature being everywhere music, if you can only reach it.

Hendrix, with his melodious apocalyptic nature, has held a rank among us, his function as the hero taken as divinity, the hero taken as prophet, then next the hero taken as poet. We took him for one divinely inspired, as a poet, a beautiful verse-maker, and a man of genius. This was like a first-hand glance into the very essence of things. Poetic genius, of whatsoever is best and truest, were visible in this man. A strong, wild man—a man who shaped himself into poet, king, priest and hero.

The first full-fledged American tour by the Jimi Hendrix Experience opened at Arizona State University on 7 February 1968. Four days later, Hendrix returned to Seattle. He hadn't seen his father for seven years. He had left Garfield High School without graduating, and now the school board fell all over themselves, giving him an honorary diploma. The returning hero. The prodigal son. A sell-out show at the Seattle Center Arena. And he hadn't been in Seattle for, as he put it, 'five thousand years.'

Above: Jimi, along with Noel Redding and Leonard Nimoy (*center*) at a Cleveland, Ohio press conference in March 1968. The 37-year-old Nimoy had last performed in his role as 'Mr Spock' two years before when the *Star Trek* television series was canceled, and had recently appeared in the film *Valley of Mystery*. Jimi was at the apogee of his career.

Facing page: Jimi played Brown University in Providence, Rhode Island on 8 March 1968.

The tour was incredible. Everything that could happen, happened. Superlatives became understatements. The Shrine Auditorium in Los Angeles on 16 February. Dallas on 22 February. Chicago on 27 February. New York on 29 February. Columbus on 3 March. Back to New York City.

By the summer of 1968, Hendrix had moved into the Drake Hotel in New York with a restless woman known as Devon and began working on what was to be the next album for the Experience. He hung out in a boutique on East Ninth Street with a woman from North Africa named Monique. He played wild, weird jams at nightclubs like the Scene with people like Jeff Beck, Buddy Miles and the Chambers Brothers. He sat in with Howlin' Wolf. Meanwhile, *Electric Ladyland*, his third album in less than two years, was taking shape at the state-of-the-art studio known simply as the Record Plant.

He met Janis Joplin, that strange woman from Port Arthur, Texas with whose fate his own was inextricably linked. They sang and played the blues. It was a wild and unpredictable time. They are said to have shared the spotlight at a fabulous concert at Forest Hills on Long Island and a fifth of Jack Daniels backstage afterward. Hendrix commuted to Los Angeles to hang out with Buddy Miles, Stephen Stills and numerous ladies who made his home their home away from home and who made Jimi's stay in the Hollywood Hills a memorable one. He also recorded in Los Angeles on the wonderful 16-track machines that were placed at his disposal whenever he came within a block of a studio.

Electric Ladyland debuted on 2 November 1968. It hit number one on the American charts immediately. The album's highlights included *Voodoo Chile*, *Crosstown Traffic* and a cover of Bob Dylan's *All Along the Watchtower*. *All Along the Watchtower* was so good that Dylan himself borrowed Jimi's arrangement when he finally went back on the road in 1974.

At the end of 1968, the Experience returned to London in triumph for the first time in 18 months, but it was clear that

Above: **Hendrix found a kindred spirit in Janis Joplin. They met at the Monterey Pop Festival and later shared the stage at a legendary concert in Forest Hills, New York. Ironically, Joplin was found dead within a week of Jimi's death three years later.**

Above left and facing page: **On vinyl and on stage, the Jimi Hendrix of 1968 was a riveting presence.**

Noel Redding and Mitch Mitchell were itching to go their separate ways. They would not have that opportunity immediately, but their intentions would serve to darken the ambience of the coming year.

Despite this backdrop of an imminent break-up, a new world tour was planned to begin in January 1969. The tour opened in Sweden on 9 January, with the European leg highlighted by filmed performances on 18 and 24 January at the Royal Albert Hall in London for a proposed feature-length concert film. With the Experience members wanting to spread their wings, when the tour hit the United States, the opening act was Noel Redding's Fat Mattress.

In May 1969, a further blow befell Jimi when he was busted and then released for drug possession by Canadian authorities while he was en route to a show in Canada and found himself in the bizarre world of the Canadian legal system, which would continue to dog him for months.

Despite this, Jimi continued to tour, headlining for the Newport Pop Festival on 20 June. He went to Los Angeles again and was paid $125,000 for one show—the highest ever paid to a performer up to that time.

Tragedy was followed by triumph, which was followed by change. The Experience's last performance was on 29 June at the Denver Pop Festival. Shortly afterward, Noel Redding heard change was in the air and split, and the Jimi Hendrix Experience was no more. Mitchell would drift back into the fold periodically, but it was over. A turning point had been reached.

There was no shortage of musical acquaintances in Jimi's circle, so it was only a question of *who*, and the answer to this question would define the 'Hendrix sound' for the next kaleidoscopic months.

Nothing immediately gelled. Hendrix had to prepare for Woodstock, so he escaped to upstate New York to find himself. He called on an old Army friend, Billy Cox, to play bass. He called Mitchell back to play drums. Loose jams ensued with the likes of percussionist Juma Sultan, guitarist Larry Lee and pianist Mike Ephron, among others.

They all hung out around Woodstock, a resort town upstate from New York City that had become a sort of rest stop for restless rockers after Bob Dylan had semi-retired there following his near-fatal motorcycle crash in the summer of 1966. Dylan and the Band lived there. So did Paul Butterfield and his entourage. Mike Bloomfield and his crowd passed through. It was like San Francisco in 1967, but with a distinctly rural flavor. Occasionally they'd slide down to the Record Plant in Manhattan to lay down a few tracks and then drift back to Woodstock to hang out under the trees to create and recreate.

Many musicians dream of having their own recording

These pages: **For Jimi Hendrix, the formative years were over by 1968. He was on the threshold of a turning point in his life. Soon he would change, but still he was the introspective genius, at one with the inner structure of nature. The soul of all his voices and utterances was inherent in his perfect music.**

Above: The poster advertising a 1969 Jimi Hendrix Experience appearance in Indianapolis, Indiana.

Below: A quarter of a million people flocked to Max Yasgur's farm in upstate New York to take part in the 'Aquarian Exposition' remembered today simply as 'Woodstock.'

studio. Not just a room with some Belgian rugs on the wall and a reel-to-reel, but a *real*, full-fledged *studio* with 16-track and 32-track machines and bells and whistles. Most musicians can't afford such a luxury. The Beatles could, and began building one in the Apple Corps building. Others continued to dream about one. Not Jimi.

He didn't want to deal with the whims of the guy who controlled scheduling at the Record Plant. This didn't suit his creative ethos. He wanted to record when he wanted to record. He had to have his own place. He decided to follow the lead of the Beatles and build his own studio. It would be called Electric Lady Studios. Located on West Eighth Street in Greenwich Village, it was in the nucleus of the club district. Electric Lady became the hive around which the Band of Gypsys would swarm in the summer of 1969.

The summer of 1967, when the sixties really began, was the Summer of Love. The summer of 1969, which serves to define our memory of the sixties, was the summer of Woodstock. It was billed as the 'Woodstock Music & Art Fair Presents An Aquarian Exposition in White Lake, New York. . . . three days of Peace and Music' to be held 15, 16 and 17 August 1969. The world remembers the music, and the gathering was generally peaceful. The world doesn't remember Wallkill, New York, where it was supposed to be held, nor the community of White Lake near Bethell, where it was actually held. The world remembers Woodstock. Few people remember that it was called 'Woodstock' because Bob Dylan was supposed to live in Woodstock and the promoters hoped that the Dylan mystique would help to sell tickets, which ranged in price from $7.00 for one day to $18.00 for all three days.

The promoters rented Max Yasgur's Bethell farm for $50,000, so they needed roughly 4000 people to break even on that expense, but they sold 186,000 tickets and banked over two million dollars. Then they had to pay the acts.

By the eve of the first day, there were 25,000 people camping on or near the Yasgur farm, but most of them had drifted in through other people's farms without paying any admission, and it was clear that they'd come to stay until the festival was over. By the time the festival opened at the end of the afternoon on 15 August, every highway for miles had been stilled by gridlock. Thousands of cars idled in the muggy 90-degree heat of the upstate New York summer.

Meanwhile, at Yasgur's farm an estimated 400,000 people sat or stood shoulder to shoulder in the dirt, watching and waiting. Those around the periphery could come and go to the portable toilets, but those with the 'best seats' for the show

Above: The Jimi Hendrix Experience in concert. The group's last performance together was at Denver's Mile High Stadium on 29 June 1969.

Right: After the Experience went their separate ways, Jimi retreated to a rural home near Woodstock, New York where he began making music with a loose group of musicians which included his old friend Billy Cox.

were literally adrift in the biggest sea of humanity in memory. The situation would remain the same for the next three days, except that the rain would turn the dirt to mud, and the unmet sanitary needs of a quarter million people who couldn't move would turn the scene into a bizarre, almost medieval, amalgam of heaven and hell. Heaven for the sake of the best musical show most people would ever experience in their lifetimes and hell for what they would have to endure in order to experience it.

Some people escaped and went home, but most stayed. But for those who stayed, it was like a dream come true.

We dream of an immortal life here on Earth, but we don't stop to consider the limitations, the conditions, of such a life, even were it possible. Even if we could live here forever on this Earth and all be healthy and strong, if we could gain what is at present an almost unimaginable control over the native forces of the Earth, would we believe it to be true?

How much of what makes up the happiness of life was present in this dream world?

Dreamers dreamed. They dreamed those special dreams that dreamers first started dreaming in the sixties.

Friday night's line-up made it look like a folk festival: Joan Baez, Arlo Guthrie, Tim Hardin and even Ravi Shankar. Except for Sly and the Family Stone, the rockers didn't arrive until Saturday. Saturday's show presented a pantheon of sixties rock—West Coast style: Credence Clearwater Revival, the Grateful Dead, Jefferson Airplane and the queen herself, Janis Joplin. It was almost like Monterey Pop two years and so, so many light years before. In 1967, the popularity of the Monterey Pop Festival took the world by surprise, but Woodstock was an opportunity for *everyone* to make the scene once before the sixties ended. Nearly half a million did.

The Who climaxed Saturday's show, but rumors rippled through the audience about those who had not shown but whose presence was still felt like the electricity of distant lightning. Where were the stars at the apex of the pantheon? Would they show or not?

Bob Dylan lived near enough to hear the festival, but he never ventured to Yasgur's farm.

The Rolling Stones were in London. They sat out Woodstock, regretted it, tried to recreate it in California at Altamont four months later and failed miserably.

The Beatles hadn't been on a stage in three years, and for all intents and purposes, they had already broken up and would never be a group again.

That left Jimi Hendrix.

He was scheduled to be on Woodstock's stage Sunday. Not before. Jimi would play *last*. Ever since Monterey, no performer dared to *follow* Hendrix.

Facing page: Photographers swarm as Jimi Hendrix plugs in his Fender Stratocaster on-stage at Woodstock on 18 August 1969.

Above: Hendrix lost in thought amidst the swirling masses at Woodstock.

Hendrix took the stage after Jeff Beck, Joe Cocker, Johnny Winter, Ten Years After and Iron Butterfly. He followed Crosby, Stills & Nash, the hottest American band playing in the summer of 1969 and the Band, Bob Dylan's back-up group.

The rains and extended line-up of acts would have ended up putting Hendrix on stage at about 3 am. He refused and said he would play at daybreak. It was 8:30 am on Monday morning. Jefferson Airplane awoke the remaining crowd for Hendrix, who was dressed in a white leather jacket with beaded fringe. He greeted the crowd with nearly two hours of long- awaited karma. He had been in town for three sleepless days jamming with the band that would back his historic moment at Woodstock: Billy Cox on bass, Larry Lee on guitar, Mitch Mitchell on drums, Juma Sultan on congas and Jerry Velez on percussion.

Jimi struck the first crisp notes of *Purple Haze* and the audience shrieked. They became one with the spirit of the moment, at one with Jimi Hendrix. With bursting earnestness, with a fierce, savage sincerity, articulating in that heaven and that hell, he was the natural voice of humanity and the heart of a wild son of nature. Jimi's paradise was sensual, his hell sensual. In the one and the other there was that which shocks all the spiritual feeling in us.

Purple Haze was like an anthem. What could follow it but another anthem? *The* anthem. Nobody *ever* played the *Star Spangled Banner* like Hendrix, and he never played the *Star Spangled Banner* like he did on 18 August 1969. It is only when the heart of him is rapt into true passion of melody, and the very tones of him become musical by the greatness, depth and music of his thoughts, that we can give him the right to rhyme and sing; that we call him a poet, and listen to him as the most heroic of speakers—whose speech *is song*. Pretenders to this are many. Rhyme that has no inward necessity to be rhymed—it ought to have told us plainly, without any jingle, what it was aiming at. Precisely, as we love the true song and are charmed by it as by something divine, so shall we hate the false song, and account it a mere wooden noise, a thing hollow, superfluous and altogether an insincere and offensive thing.

After Woodstock, Hendrix canceled several major dates, but played a street fair in Harlem, a curious paradox for a black artist who was so popular among white audiences yet estranged from the black soul and rhythm & blues mainstream.

What had been born at Monterey and the Human Be-In in 1967 was a magic thing, and that magic thing was an epoch known as the sixties. When people today talk about the sixties,

Above: Hendrix performing at another memorable outdoor event of 1969—the Newport Pop Festival, Los Angeles.

Facing page: Jimi Hendrix during his Woodstock performance, plucking the guitar strings with his teeth.

Below: Two Woodstock audience members enjoy a refreshing dip in a nearby river.

ARE YOU EXPERIENCED?

Left: Jimi Hendrix on stage at the Woodstock Music & Art Fair on 18 August 1969. He was supposed to have played on 17 August, but rain delayed his appearance. He struck the first crisp notes of *Purple Haze* and the audience shrieked. They became one with the spirit of the moment, at one with Jimi Hendrix. With bursting earnestness, with a fierce, savage sincerity, articulating in that heaven and that hell, he was the natural voice of humanity and the heart of a wild son of nature. Jimi's paradise was sensual, his hell sensual. In the one and the other there was that which shocks all the spiritual feeling in us.

Above: **Hendrix at the Newport Pop Festival. Jimi played a second unscheduled set at the festival to make up for what he considered a poor initial performance.**

they are talking about a span of time that lasted less than three years. Nevertheless, the sixties are as important to Western cultural history as epochs like the Middle Ages or the Renaissance.

The magic born in 1967 could not evolve beyond Woodstock. The festival for 400,000 people at Yasgur's farm was the climax, and the beginning of the end. The end would come four months later in December when the Rolling Stones tried to recreate Woodstock at the Altamont Speedway east of San Francisco.

Woodstock embodied the spirit of 'peace and love.' Altamont was the Hell's Angels, beatings and a murder barely 20 feet from where Mick Jagger stood singing *Sympathy for the Devil*. The sixties were essentially over after Woodstock, and they died in the dirt at Altamont.

The years after 1969 were to be the period in history when the priests had succeeded in transforming the power of nature into a highly artificial system of rites, ceremonies and sacrifices. They were always intent upon deepening their hold on the minds of the people, by surrounding their own vocation with the halo of sanctity and divine inspiration. With them it was a matter of position and influence and money, like the televangelists who continue to urge the necessity of frequent and liberal offerings to the gods, and to invoke worldly blessings upon devotees.

Unfortunately, when belief becomes uncertain, practice too becomes unsound, and errors, injustices and miseries everywhere more and more prevail, we shall see material enough for our new spiritual revolution. Elvis' sublime work, incredible now in nostalgia but defaced in the sixties, was torn asunder by a Hendrix. Even the Beatles' noble work, as beautiful as it once looked and was, ended in their own bickering and was in turn buried by disco, by new wave and then by rap. When the sixties were gasping their last breath, Jimi Hendrix was in Toronto facing a Canadian judge and the possibility of several years in jail for his May 1969 drug bust.

Bill Graham, the San Francisco rock promoter who had started booking shows in 1966 at the old Fillmore Auditorium, later went on to create what were to be the Valhallas of rock in the 1967-1969 period. These were the Fillmore West in San Francisco (much bigger than the old Fillmore Auditorium) and the Fillmore East on New York's Lower East Side. Everybody who was somebody—and everybody who wasn't as well— wanted to play 'the Fillmore'—*either* Fillmore.

The Grateful Dead always played the Fillmore West on New Year's Eve, but the shows at the Fillmore East varied. For 31 December 1969, the figurative and literal end of the sixties, Bill Graham wanted no less a figure than Jimi Hendrix on

stage at the Fillmore East. Hendrix agreed that he and his Band of Gypsys—Bill Cox on bass and Buddy Miles on drums—would play two shows each on 31 December 1969 and 1 January 1970. The result would be preserved forever in the live album *Band of Gypsys*.

It was awesome. It was another milestone. It was definitely quintessential Hendrix, the essence of life and spirit.

From the spiritual standpoint, we know that often what is real to the spirit is not real to the human senses. We could neither see, nor feel, nor touch, nor taste, nor smell, nor would any material sense enable us to perceive the spirit realm in any manner whatever. When we perceive the spirit realm, the realm that 'the eye has not seen and the ear has not heard,' it is the realm of spirit known by perception.

There are millions of vibrations of sounds which do not come within the range of our physical ears. If we could hear all the great sounds, we would be deaf to ordinary sounds. Our eyes are not attuned to the many vibrations of light. They have but a limited range in the scale of light. There are numberless vibrations of light which we do not see at all. So with every physical sense.

The next, and final, Jimi Hendrix tour began on 25 April 1970 at the Forum in Inglewood, California. The tour was to last just over three months and culminate in his fourth studio album—his first in over a year—tentatively titled *First Rays of The New Rising Sun*.

Above: Jimi's first post-Experience group, The Band of Gypsys, featured Buddy Miles *(left)* on drums and Billy Cox *(right)* on bass.

Below: Accompanied by two friends, Hendrix revels in his relief and happiness after being acquitted on charges of drug possession on 10 December 1969.

THE HIGHWAY CHILD

The law is coldest steel,
We live beneath its sway,
It cares not what we feel,
And so pass night and day.

T he dawn of the 1970s found Jimi Hendrix feeling listless and disconnected. It was the mood of a generation. The war that raged in Southeast Asia was mirrored by the war that raged on America's streets.

Woodstock had been an altar to peace and love, but by the spring of 1970, there was no peace and there was little love. The Woodstock nation was at war with the United States, and the United States was at war with Vietnam.

The Ohio National Guard had fired on war protesters at Kent State University and there were mobs running riot on campuses throughout the land. The weather was good and the specters that haunted the periphery of the college scene were inspiring students to move into the warm spring nights and make their voices heard. Nowhere was this more true than at the University of California, Berkeley. The city of Berkeley had always been a strange place, an otherworldly haven for alternative life-styles—so long as they were left of center—and alternative political doctrines—so long as they were left of center. In May 1970, Berkeley was on fire with the People's Park riots, and clouds of tear gas drifted in the streets.

Into this maelstrom came Jimi Hendrix. Bill Graham, with either uncanny ignorance or an incredible sense of the dramatic, had booked the wild man of rock into the Berkeley Community Theater.

As crowds bashed windows in the distance, Hendrix *opened* with the *Star Spangled Banner*.

It was September 1814, 160 years before. England and the United States—not Vietnam and the United States—were at war, and a powerful British fleet, carrying thousands of soldiers, had arrived in Chesapeake Bay. Five thousand British troops, landing at a point on the Patuxent River, a tributary of Chesapeake Bay 20 miles from Washington, advanced on the city, and, after forcing President Madison, his cabinet and other officials to flee, they burned the capitol and the White House, and ransacked other public buildings.

Meanwhile, detained on a small vessel, the *Minden*, among the British ships, was a lawyer from Georgetown named Francis Scott Key, who had only a few days before seen the capital looted. As an official envoy, he had gone to see the British admiral when the fleet was in the Patuxent River, regarding the release of an aged American doctor, an intimate friend, who was being held prisoner.

Fearing that he might reveal information about the plans being made to advance on Baltimore, Key was detained aboard a British ship, to be held until after the bombardment was completed.

Watching the battle continue as night fell, Key withdrew an envelope from his pocket and began jotting down notes: 'And

Above and opposite top: **No-body *ever* played the *Star Spangled Banner* like Hendrix. It is only when the heart of him is rapt into true passion of melody, and the very tones of him become musical by the greatness, depth and music of his thoughts, that we can give him the right to rhyme and sing; that we call him a poet, and listen to him as the most heroic of speakers—whose speech is *song*. Hendrix had taken so unlikely a song as the American national anthem, and he had made it *his* anthem. Francis Scott Key meet James Marshall Hendrix.**

the rocket's red glare, the bombs bursting in air,' he wrote, 'gave proof through the night that our flag was still there!'

At midnight, there was a lull in the battle, and the British learned that the land attack during the day had failed and that the British commander had been killed. In desperation, the fleet moved nearer and redoubled its fire. The fort answered, gun for gun. In the wee hours of the morning, the bombardment finally ceased, and in the silence and darkness, Francis Scott Key anxiously wondered if the flag was still intact. At last, at daybreak, his eager eyes peered through the morning mist, straining to see the low fort. Again, he took out his pencil, and, by the first light of the morning, he wrote:

'O, say can you see, by the dawn's early light,
What so proudly we hail'd at the twilight's last gleaming.

Whose broad stripes and bright stars through the perilous fight. O'er the ramparts we watched, were so gallantly streaming?'

Hendrix played Key's masterpiece with a vast sense of harmonic ironies. The anthem became an anti-anthem, a mirror image of the anthem. A mirror held up to the face of the nation. Fort McHenry, meet Hanoi. Anno 1814, meet anno 1970.

Francis Scott Key, meet James Marshall Hendrix.

Key's anthem met with Jimi's anthem and the *Star Spangled Banner* suddenly became *Purple Haze*.

'The rockets' red glare. . . . purple haze all in my eyes . . . by the dawn's early light . . . don't know if it's day or night. Let me stand next to your fire!'

In the ancient books of India, Agni, the god of fire, is addressed as the supreme god who created all things. He is represented by the light of the sun, the flashing lightning and the clear flame. He is the guardian of the sacrifice, and comprehends within himself a multitude of other deities, as the circumference of a wheel embraces its spokes. From his body issue seven streams of glory, and in his right hand he holds a spear, while a tongue of fire issues from his mouth.

In the mythology of the Vedas, Rudra is the god, or rather the *gods*, of wind and storm, to whom the people prayed for protection for themselves and for the destruction of their enemies. They were addressed as 'shakers of the Earth,' and sought to tear in pieces whatever fiends might be aroused to attack the people. They dash through the heavens in chariots drawn by dappled deer. They are termed 'worshipful and wise,' and implored to come with their whole help 'as quickly as lightnings come after rain.' Rudra was afterward the god of destruction—Siva, the world dissolver. The active, the strong, the singers, the never flinching, the immovable, the wild, the most beloved and most manly, they have shown themselves with their glittering ornaments like only the heavens with stars.

Hendrix closed out the sixties by digging back to his African American roots. Calling on old friends—bassist Billy Cox and drummer Buddy Miles—he created the Band of Gypsys. Unlike the Experience, they were a band, not of gypsies but of Americans—African Americans. Though the Band of Gypsys was distinctly different from the Experience both ethnically and musically, the driving force was still the same left-handed dude with the right-handed Fender Stratocaster.

The Band of Gypsys closed the sixties with four shows New Year's Eve and New Year's Day at the Fillmore East in New York. Heralded as one of the most significant performances in rock history, Hendrix rang out the old with his own rendition of *Auld Lang Syne* while introducing an entirely new brand of music. It was as if he was telling us the psychedelic Sixties were over. But Hendrix met opposition from his all black entourage.

His management didn't like the direction, since Hendrix attracted predominantly white crowds. The Black Panthers approached Hendrix to become more involved with their organization—whose philosophy Hendrix rejected because he believed all people were of the same color. Ultimately, the continuing three-piece band format failed, as it imposed limitations on Hendrix's music.

As Hendrix moved into 1970, he rambled and searched for musicians to help fulfill his musical fantasies. He hung out in New York City with the avant garde jazz set—Rahsaan Rolan Kirk, Larry Young, John McLaughlin and Taj Mahal.

He needed to continue to tour to pay his way, so he called back Mitch Mitchell to team this time with Band of Gypsys' bassist Billy Cox. But he still wanted more.

Miraculously, the 30 May 1970 Berkeley concert was captured on film for posterity as the unambiguously titled *Jimi Plays Berkeley*. However, the Berkeley show was not to be the cinematically preserved swansong.

Less than two months later, the Band of Gypsys performed in Haleakala Crater on the Hawaiian Island of Maui, where Warner Brothers filmed Jimi's concert in this ethereal setting of the Rainbow Bridge Occult Center with their drug-oriented, stream-of-consciousness philosophies.

The band now featured those two solid standbys—Billy Cox on bass and the old Experience drummer, Mitch Mitchell. Together they constructed the last cinematic testament of the voodoo child.

The show was billed as the Rainbow Bridge Vibratory Color-Sound Experiment. That suited him. It seemed as though everything about Jimi was experimental. He was the Great Experimenter. It was as though the day came when matter and force were in the right space so that the Great Experimenter

Below: Hendrix in a happy moment during the post-Woodstock autumn of 1969.

could wield intelligence and energy enough to prepare a speck of protoplasm consisting of matter, force and intelligence, with intelligence predominating.

Its potency was still an unknown quantity, but it already had certain fixed qualities. Not having access to any celestial dictionary, it contained an infusion of intelligence that permitted it to attract and select other atoms, and therein was a field of unknown possibilities—in fact, a whole world full of them. It could multiply and increase cells indefinitely, if only it could attract the requisite matter and force. From the very first, it could use its intelligence to make choices and wield its power of repulsion to drive off atoms not adapted to its use. 'Lately, things just don't seem the same . . . . acting funny, but I don't know why. 'Scuse me while I kiss the sky.'

Life had now reached that point at which history might commence. The Great Experimenter had himself a lesson to learn before he could progress much further. His wondrous cell could manufacture more cells like itself, but it soon grew unwieldy, so it would split in two, or a dozen. Here was what we might call a species of immortality that nothing but catastrophe could destroy. Apparently long ages passed before the Great Experimenter discerned the cause of the trouble. Matter and force were more than holding their own against intelligence. There must be a radical change, or further progress was impossible. At last he returned to his primal protoplasm and laid down a rule for his future guidance. The single cell was to be the starting point as before, but progress demanded that every form dominated by intelligence should have the same starting point. The conditions under which the wondrous protoplasm was formed had changed.

'Is it tomorrow, or just the end of time?'

Back in New York by midsummer, Jimi completed his first full session at the Electric Lady Studios on 1 July, recording a song that had been taking shape in his mind since Mick Jagger moved in on the woman named Devon who had been Jimi's love interest for nearly a year.

Dolly Dagger concerns a woman who had 'been riding broomsticks since she was 15, blowing out all the other witches on the scene. . . . . Her tongue can even scratch the soul out of the devil's wife.' The song is a thinly disguised portrait of Devon who, in Hendrix's insinuation, 'drinks her blood from a jagged edge.'

'Drink up, baby,' Jimi had added.

First Rays of The New Rising Sun was to be the first full album recorded at Electric Lady. It was to be ethereal and metaphysical, the voice of a man in search of the rest of his life, a searcher who would ultimately fail. 'There must be some kinda way outta here!' said the Joker to the Thief.

After the Electric Lady recording sessions, Hendrix, with Cox and Mitchell by his side, resumed the tour that they had begun the spring before. It was the European leg of the tour that took Jimi back to England for the first time in well over a year. He never returned to America alive.

Jimi played the Isle of Wight Festival, a British Woodstock in the sense that Woodstock was an East Coast Monterey. He opened his set with *God Save the Queen*, a parody of his own parody of the *Star Spangled Banner* in Berkeley. Between 31 August and 3 September, the Gypsys played four dates in Scandinavia before moving on to Berlin, where Hendrix was greeted like a deity.

By mid-September, an exhausted Jimi Hendrix was back in London renewing his former relationship with Monika Danne-

Above: **The dawn of the 1970s found Jimi feeling listless and disconnected. It was the mood of a generation. The war that raged in Southeast Asia was mirrored by the war that raged on America's streets.**

Facing page: **Hendrix often performed for friends at private parties—on guitar and sometimes piano.**

Above: **Drummer Mitch Mitchell rejoined Hendrix for Jimi's last tour which began with a show at the Inglewood Forum, California on 25 April 1970.**

man. Their reunion was complicated by the arrival from New York of the jealous Devon, and the final act was set in motion.

It had become evident to him that he no longer had any resting place, or hope of benefit, on this Earth. The earthly world had cast him forth, to wander. There was no living heart to love him now. For his sore miseries there was no solace here.

Hendrix had met Monika Danneman in Germany in 1968, and they remained in touch by telephone and letter while he was in the States. Jimi began staying with Monika at 22 Landsdowne Crescent in London on Tuesday, 15 September 1970. She noted that he took sleeping tablets from his doctor 'because he was nervous,' but he had insisted they were 'not that strong.' Danneman said later that she had not known Jimi to take hard drugs, but that he 'tried them once, just for the experience.' Jimi slept well on Tuesday and Wednesday nights, and on Thursday the two of them arrived back at the flat about 8:30 pm. Danneman cooked a meal and they shared a bottle of white wine about 11:00 pm. Hendrix drank more of the bottle than she did, but he had nothing to drink other than the wine. Jimi left for a brief while to go to a friend's party, returning to Danneman's apartment around 2:00 am. She recalled that there was no argument or stress. It was just a 'happy atmosphere.' Monika took a sleeping pill around 7:00 am and made some fish sandwiches.

When she awoke around 10:20 am, Jimi was sleeping normally. She went around the corner to get cigarettes, and when she came back, he had been vomiting. He was breathing and his pulse was normal but she could not wake him. She saw that he had taken the sleeping pills. Monika later reported at the official inquiry that nine pills were missing from the Vesparax bottle. 'I think he knew exactly what he could take in the way of sleeping tablets,' she said. 'When I last saw him before he went to sleep he was very happy. The tablets were in a cupboard. He would have to get out of bed to get the tablets. As far as I know, he had not taken pep tablets. He said he had cannabis at the flat. There was no question of exhaustion on this particular evening. He was not a man to have moods. He was not tense or agitated. I have never heard him say he wished he were dead or that life was not worth living. He had business stress, but this did not worry him.'

He had struck the chords on his Stratocaster, and with blow after blow his ax had echoed through the world. Suddenly, he reeled in pain and cried. At her side Monika saw a fearful shape, that was neither god nor man. Tall and dark with a grim visage, he looked down pitilessly. His garments were crimson as if with blood. His eyes glowed like burning coals in their deep sockets. The trembling woman laid her head ten-

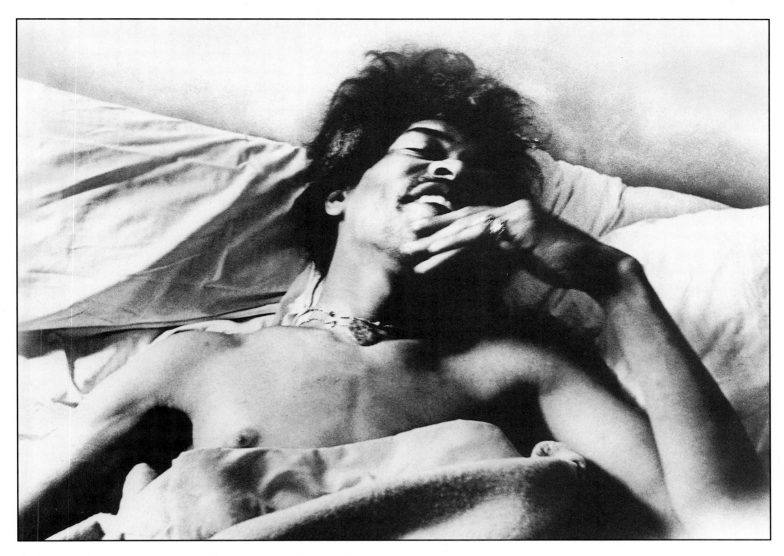

Above: **James Marshall Hendrix died on 18 September 1970. Although it was known that Hendrix was going through some troubling times, those who knew Jimi rule out the possibility of suicide.**

derly upon the ground, and springing up, reverently folded her hands in supplication, and asked him who he was and why he came. He answered, 'I am Yama, the god of death, and I have come to bear away the soul of Jimi Hendrix.'

'But,' pleaded Monika, 'isn't it your messengers who take away the souls of men? Why is it that you have come?'

'Because *he* was the grandest, noblest of all,' replied the god, 'and none save Yama's self is worthy to bear his spirit to the other side.'

Monika phoned for an ambulance, and Jimi was taken to St Mary's Abbot Hospital in Kensington, where he was pro-nounced dead on arrival. At 11:25 am on 18 September 1970, Jimi Hendrix was pronounced dead. Newspapers and wire ser-vices reported worldwide that Hendrix had died of a drug over-dose, but the death certificate listed the exact cause of death as: 'Inhalation of vomit, quinalbarbitone intoxication. Insuffi-cient evidence of circumstances. Open verdict.' Curiously, Gavin LB Thurston, the coroner for Inner West London, did not sign the death certificate.

'Purple haze all in my eyes, don't know if it's day or night. You got me going, blowing my mind. Is it tomorrow or just the end of time?'

When Jimi Hendrix died, he had four albums in print. Who could have imagined that a quarter century later those four would be selling as well—if not better—than they did in 1970, and that they would have been joined by over a hundred other albums featuring live performances and studio tracks that had not been released before his death?

Jimi died, but his popularity never has. It continues to grow.

Al Hendrix inherited his son's estate, which was—and still is—managed by entertainment attorney Leo Branton. In 1972, it was sold for an undisclosed sum to a Panamanian holding company called PMSA.

Although the 'estate' has been sold and resold several times since, Jimi's father continues to receive a modest residual that Branton arranged for him in the early 1970s. The other members of the Jimi Hendrix Experience also cashed in their shares. Noel Redding earned $100,000 and Mitch Mitchell was paid $300,000.

Above: **His grave site at Mount Greenwood in Renton, Washington, south of Seattle, still receives almost daily visits from fans loyal to his memory.**

Facing page: **A moody Jimi, the way we want to remember him, with his mighty guitar in hand.**

AND THE WIND CRIES JIMI

And we are weak as waves
That sink upon the shore;
We go down into graves—
Fate chants the nevermore.

Although everyone realized that Jimi's popularity would never die, no one had any idea that it would grow as big as it ultimately did. In the early 1990s, four million Hendrix disks—vinyl and CD—were being sold worldwide annually, with a quarter of those in the United States alone, an utterly staggering amount for a man who went to his grave with only four albums in the stores. These sales, plus those of videos of his filmed concerts, continue to net the owners of his 'estate' approximately $3 million every year. A quarter century after his death, Jimi Hendrix was more popular than most of the artists who were alive and still producing new material. As one commentator asked rhetorically, 'I wonder whether Madonna and Michael Jackson will be averaging a million units a year on each of their albums in 2005?' Probably not. Jimi Hendrix did not desert us. His albums and his music distinguished themselves by their sublime and exultant tone. There was an absence of fear which arises through thought or affection and which counteracts the presence of hatred and stupid fury. No accusation could be more unjust than the accusations of malevolence that were brought against him. He had a most gentle heart, full of pity and love, as indeed the truly valiant heart always is. Between him and his fans there was an ether like the ether between heaven and Earth. In this ether the breath is fixed, as in that other ether the air is fixed. As there is lightning in the sky, there is his heart in the body and a memory that never dies.

Doubtless it would be finer today if we could go along always in the way of *music*, to be tamed and taught by our poets as the people of the sixties were. But it is not so. The battling performer too is, from time to time, a needful and inevitable phenomenon.

It cannot be that our life is cast up by the ocean of eternity to float for a moment upon its waves and then sink into nothingness. Why else is it that the glorious aspirations, which leap like angels from the temple of our hearts, are forever wandering about unsatisfied? And the wind whispers . . . 'Jimi.'

Why is it that the rainbow and clouds and the purple haze come over us with a beauty that is not of Earth, and pass off to leave us to muse upon their favored loveliness? Why is it that the stars who hold their festival around the midnight throne are set above the grasp of our limited faculties, forever mocking us with their unapproachable glory? And the wind screams . . .

'Jimi.' Finally, why is it that the bright forms of human beauty are presented to our view, and then taken away from us, leaving the thousand streams of affection to flow back in alpine torrents upon our hearts? We are born for a higher destiny than that of Earth. There is a realm where the rainbow never fades, where the stars will be spread before us like islands that slumber on the ocean and where the beings that pass before us like shadows shall stay in our presence forever. And the wind cries . . . 'Jimi.'

Left: An early photo of the Jimi Hendrix Experience, January 1967. They are *(left to right)* Noel Redding, Mitch Mitchell and Jimi Hendrix.

Above: As a new band hungry for exposure, the Experience made many appearances on British television programs.

Right: Jimi, as his friends like to remember him—happy and relaxed.

JIMI HENDRIX DISCOGRAPHY

(Updated February 1, 1993. © 1993 Jimi Hendrix Information Management Institute. Used with permission.)

Jimi Hendrix US Albums Discography

Reprise RS 6261	Are You Experienced	1967 (May)
Reprise RS 6281	Axis: Bold As Love	1968
Capitol STAO 472	Band Of Gypsys	1970 (May)
Capitol SJ-12416	Band Of Gypsys 2	1986 (Sept.)
Reprise MS2204	Crash Landing	1975 (February)
Reprise MS2034	Cry Of Love	1970 (December)
Rykodisc RCD31008	Daytripper	1988 (November)
Celluloid CEL 166	Doriella Du Fontaine	1984
Restless 72663-2	Doriella Du Fontaine (CD)	1993
Reprise 2RS 6307	Electric Ladyland	1968 (September)
Rhino R2-70771	Hendrix Speaks	1990
Reprise RS 2049	In The West	1972 (February)
Reprise 25358-1	Jimi Plays Monterey	1986
Capitol MLP 15022	Johnny B. Goode	1986 (June)
Reprise 25119-1	Kiss The Sky	1985
Reprise 26435	Lifelines	1990
Rykodisc 20038	Live At Winterland	1987
Rykodisc 90038	Live At Winterland +3: The Ultimate Collection	1992
Reprise MS2229	Midnight Lightning	1975 (November)
Reprise MS2029	Monterey International Pop Fest	1970 (July)
Rhino 70596	Monterey International Pop Festival	1992
Reprise HS 2299	Nine To The Universe	1980 (April)
Rykodisc RCD20078	Radio One	1988 (November)
Reprise MS2040	Rainbow Bridge	1971 (October)
Polydor 2310 268	Smash Hits	1969 (June)
Reprise 2RS 6481	Soundtrack From The Film Jirni Hendrix	1973 (June)
Reprise 26732-2	Stages	1991
Reprise 2RS 2245	The Essential Jimi Hendrix	1978
Reprise HS 2293	The Essential Jimi Hendrix, Volume Two	1979
Columbia BL 30808	The First Great Rock Festivals Of The 70s	1972
Reprise 22306-1	The Jimi Hendrix Concerts	1982 (September)
Hal Leonard 00660040	Variations On A Theme: Red House	1989
Reprise MS2103	War Heroes	1972 (November)
Cotillion SD-3-500	Woodstock	1970
Cotillion SD-2-400	Woodstock Two	1971

European and Foreign Jimi Hendrix Album Discography

(Note: UK releases listed if different titles than US releases. All titles are UK releases unless otherwise noted)

Polydor 2494 326	A Arte De Jimi Hendrix (Brazil)	
Polydor	Al Principio Jimi Hendrix (Argentina)	
Polydor PZCD 100	All Along The Watchtower	1990
Polydor 879 583-2	All Along The Watchtower (France)	1991
Duchesse 352 064	All The Hits (Holland)	1990
Polydor 184 085	Are You Experienced (Germany)	1967 (May)
Polydor P33P 50036	Are You Experienced (Japan)	
Polydor P20P-22001	Are You Experienced (Japan)	
Polydor POCP-2019	Are You Experienced (Japan)	
Polydor 2679 021	Are You Exp'd/Axis: Bold As Love	
Fontana 9294900	Attention	1978
Polydor	Axis: Bold As Love	1967 (December)
Polydor P33P 25023	Axis: Bold As Love (Japan)	
Polydor P20P-22002	Axis: Bold As Love (Japan)	
Polydor POCP-2020	Axis: Bold As Love (Japan)	

UFO 1-873884-03-5	Axis: Bold As Love—	1992	Music Gala/Arcade ADEH 430		Jimi Hendrix—The Legend (Holland)	1986
	Jimi Hendrix Experience In 1967		Barclay SD587-588		Jimi Hendrix / 4	
Track 2407 001	Backtrack 1	1970 (May)	Barclay 80555		Jimi Plays Berkeley	1977
Track 2407 002	Backtrack 2	1970 (May)	BMG 791168		Jimi Plays Berkeley	1991
Track 2407 003	Backtrack 3	1970 (May)	Polydor		Jimi Plays Monterey (Footlights box)	1991
Track 99 2407 004	Backtrack 4	1970 (May)	Polydor P33P 25003		Jimi Plays Monterey (Japan)	
Track 2407 005	Backtrack 5	1970 (May)	Polydor P20P 22015		Jimi Plays Monterey (Japan)	
Track 2407 007	Backtrack 7	1970 (November)	Polydor POCP-2026		Jimi Plays Monterey (Japan)	
Track 2407 010	Backtrack 10: Are You Experienced	1971	Monkey		Jimmy Hendrx (France)	
Track 2407 011	Backtrack 11: Axis: Bold As Love	1971	Capitol/EMI		Johnny B. Goode (Australia)	1990
Polydor	Band Of Gypsys (Footlights)	1990	Polydor P33P 50007		Kiss The Sky (Japan)	
Polydor P33P 25022	Band Of Gypsys (Japan)		Polydor P20P 22017		Kiss The Sky (Japan)	
Polydor P20P-22006	Band Of Gypsys (Japan)		Polydor POCP 2029		Kiss The Sky (Japan)	
Polydor POCP-2022	Band Of Gypsys	1991	Teichiku 30CP 232		Last Experience (Japan)	
Polydor	Battle Of Jimi Hendrix & The Who	1974	Polydor MPZ 8113/4		Legacy (Japan)	1974
Polydor 113	Best Of Jimi Hendrix (Holland)	1972	Polydor 2490 156		Legendary Jimi Hendrix (Holland)	1980
Action Replay 1022	Best Of & Rest Of Jimi Hendrix	1991	Polydor 2302 114		Live	1982
Early Years 3303	British Beat Live In Germany 1966-67	1989	DGR 1009		Live At Scene Club, New York (Holland)	1986
Univibes UV1001	Calling Long Distance	1992	Polydor 833 004-1		Live At Winterland	1987
Polydor 847 231-2	Cornerstones	1990	Polydor		Live At Winterland (Footlights box)	1991
Polydor POCP-1064	Cornerstones (Japan)	1990	Polydor P33P 20119		Live At Winterland (Japan)	
Polydor P33P 25024	Crash Landing (Japan)		Polydor P20P 22016		Live At Winterland (Japan)	
Polydor P20P-22012	Crash Landing (Japan)		Polydor POCP 2027		Live At Winterland (Japan)	
Polydor POCP-2025	Crash Landing (Japan)		Polydor 2310 301		Loose Ends	1974 (February)
Polydor P33P 25011	Cry Of Love (Japan)		Polydor P20P 22011		Loose Ends (Japan)	
Polydor P20P-22007	Cry Of Love (Japan)		Karussel		Los Three Grandes (Guatemala)	1980
Polydor POCP-2025	Cry Of Love (Japan)		Polydor 23 10 380		Lo Mejor De Jimi Hendrix	1977
Track 2856 002	Electric Hendrix	1968	Polydor		Masters Of Rock: Jimi Hendrix	1980
Polydor	Electric Ladyland	1968	Polydor		Message From Nine To The Universe	1980 (April)
Polydor P58P 25001/2	Electric Ladyland (Japan)				(Brazil)	
Polydor P36P-22004/5	Electric Ladyland (Japan)		Polydor P22P 25025		Midnight Lightning (Japan)	
Polydor POCP-2021	Electric Ladyland (Japan)		Polydor P20P 22013		Midnight Lightning (Japan)	
Ember NR5057	Experience (soundtrack)	1971	Ember NR 5061		More Experience	1972
Jimco JIM0043	Experience At Royal Albert Hall (Japan)	1990	Polydor 2675 150		Pop Giants, Volume 2	1976
Polydor 847 235-2	Footlights aka The Live Box 1990		Polydor 2675 013		Pop History, Volume 2	1984
Polydor POCP 9009/12	Footlights aka The Live Box (Japan)	1990	Teldec		Profile Of Jimi (Holland)	1984
Polydor 2141 120	Gloria	1979	Polydor PZCD33		Purple Haze	1988
Intercord	Good Times (France)	1975	Success 2101		Purple Haze (Holland)	1990
Bigtime 261 5252	Greatest Classics	1988	Castle 12001		Radio One	1989
Up	Hendrix & Youngblood (Italy)		Victor VDP 1454		Radio One (Japan)	1989
Polydor 2486 158	Hey Joe	1968	Polydor 2475 711		Rare Tracks	1971
Aquarius 67-JH-080	Historic Performances (Italy)	1990	Polydor 2679 379		Re-Experienced (Holland)	1976
Starlife 36121	In Concert	1991	Polydor		Rock Legends: Jimi Hendrix (Australia)	1980
Polydor	In The West		Polydor 2480 306		Rock 'n' Soul Sensations	1976
Polydor P33P-25004	In The West (Japan)		Polydor 847 232-2		Sessions aka The Studio Box	1990
Polydor P20P-22009	n The West (Japan)		Polydor POCP 9013/16		Sessions aka The Studio Box (Japan)	1990
Tabak CINT 5006	Introspective	1991	Polydor PODV 6		Singles Album	1983
Polydor 847 236-2	Isle Of Wight	1991	Polydor P58P 20112/3		Singles Album (Japan)	1990
Polydor 2302 016	Isle Of Wight	1971 (November)	Polydor		Smash Hits	1969
Polydor P33P 25010	Isle Of Wight (Japan)		Polydor P33P 50030		Smash Hits (Japan)	
Polydor P20P 22008	Isle Of Wight (Japan)		Polydor P20P 22030		Smash Hits (Japan)	
Polydor POCP 2028	Isle Of Wight (Japan)		Reprise K64017		Soundtrack For The Film Jimi Hendrix	1972
Polydor 847 236-2	Isle Of Wight (Footlights)	1990	Sonet SPCD-8		Spotlight	
Interpak 109	I Don't Live Today	1980	Polydor POCP 2161		Stages (Japan)	1992
Barclay 930 016-019	Jimi Hendrix (France)	1980	Polydor 2672 002		Starportrait (Germany)	1973
Polydor 2625 038	Jimi Hendrix (Holland)	1980	Polydor 2343 114		Stone Free	1980
Central CRF 009	Jimi Hendrix (Japan)	1990	Polydor		Superstarshine Vol 5 (Holland)	1973
Eyebic JECD 1030	Jimi Hendrix (Japan)	1990	Napolean		That Unforgettable Jimi Hendrix (Italy)	
World Super Hits SH1709	Jimi Hendrix (Japan)	1991	Karussell 2499 043		The Best Of Jimi Hendrix (Germany)	
Polydor POSPX401	Jimi Hendrix	1984	Polydor		The Best Of Jimi Hendrix (Germany)	1980
Polydor 2310 218	Jimi Hendrix	1974	Action CDAR 1022		The Best Of & The Rest Of Jimi Hendrix	1991
Supraphon 1 13 1384	Jimi Hendrix		Receiver		The Early Years, Live	1991
Pickwick International CN 2067	Jimi Hendrix Album	1983	Karussell		The Greatest Rock Sensation (Germany)	1976
Graffiti GR13	Jimi Hendrix Collection	1990	Pickwick International CN2067		The Jimi Hendrix Album	
Polydor	Jimi Hendrix Concerts	1990	Karussel 2499 006		The Jimi Hendrix Experience (Germany)	1976
Polydor P33P 25038	Jimi Hendrix Concerts (Japan)	1990	Bescol 42		The Last Experience (Italy)	1988
Polydor P20P 22014	Jimi Hendrix Concerts (Japan)	1991	Polydor 2490 156		The Legendary Jimi Hendrix (Holland)	1980
Polydor 2383 184	Jimi Hendrix Experience (Uruguay)	1980	Traditonal Line 1301		The New York Sessions	1989
Karussell 2499006	Jimi Hendrix Experience (Germany)	1974	Polydor 2664 379		The Story Of Jimi Hendrix (Germany)	1980
Polydor	Jimi Hendrix Live (Holland)	1982	Polydor 517 235-2		The Ultimate Experience	1992
Castle HD 100	Jimi Hendrix—Live & Unreleased	1989	Polydor 863 917-2		The Wind Cries Mary	1993
Polydor 2343 086	Jimi Hendrix, Vol 2	1976	CSJ		Two Great Experiences (Taiwan)	
Barclay 80589	Jimi Hendrix Vol 6 Greatest Hits	1975	Polydor		Very Best Of Jimi Hendrix (Japan)	
Polydor 2343 080	Jimi Hendrix, Vol 1	1975	Aero 4ADF-501		Vintage Hendrix	1983
Polydor 2343-086	Jimi Hendrix, Vol 2	1976	Karussell 2499 012		Voodoo Chile (Germany)	1973
Discussion/Merman 1983	Jimi Hendrix 1970	1991	Polydor 2343 115		Voodoo Chile	1982 (June)

Facing page: A photo from the session that produced the image used on the cover of the British version of the Experience's first album, *Are You Experienced*.

Left above: The American version of *Are You Experienced* featured a slightly different selection of songs than those on the European releases.

Above: Axis: Bold As Love, the Experience's second album, features artwork of a decidedly Eastern influence.

Left below: The Jimi Hendrix Experience's third album, *Electric Ladyland*, is considered by some to be Hendrix's magnum opus.

Polydor	War Heroes	
Polydor POCP 2024	War Heroes (Japan)	
Polydor P20P 22010	War Heroes (Japan)	
Strange Fruit 20021	Years Of Alternative Radio	1989
Polydor 822 291 30	Anos De Musica Rock (Argentina)	

Jimi Hendrix—Curtis Knight Collaborations

Produced by Ed Chalpin for PPX Productions (personnel: Curtis Knight (g), Bernard Purdie or Ray Lucas (d), Marvin Held (b)) during sessions in 1965 and 1967.

Emidisc CO48-50780	Before The Deluge (UK)	1972
Music Distributor B80045	Best Live Rarities	
MFP 50053	Birth of Success (UK)	1972
Stateside	Early Jimi Hendrix, Vol I (France)	1970
Stateside	Early Jimi Hendrix, Vol II (France)	1970
Hallmark SHM 732	Eternal Fire Of Jimi (UK)	1971
Capitol ST2894	Flashing	1968 (June)
Nardem 006	Flashing (Canada)	1981
Autograph ASK744	Flashing	
London SH 8349	Get That Feeling (UK)	1967 (December)
Capitol ST2856	Get That Feeling	1967 (December)
Capitol SWBB 659	Get That Feeling/Flashing	1971 (January)
Babylon DB80020	Guitar Giants Volume I (Holland)	1982
Babylon DB80021	Guitar Giants Volume II (Holland)	1982
Babylon DB80022	Guitar Giants Volume III (Holland)	1982
Nardem 008	Hackensack Blues (Canada)	1982
Pair SPDL2-1155	Historic Hendrix	1986 (October)
Nardem 001	Hornets Nest (Canada)	1981
Astan 201021	Hush Now (Germany)	1982
London SL 3001 1/2	In Memorium (UK)	1970
Premier CBR1031	In The Beginning (Europe)	1982
Bellaphon 1552	In The Beginning (Germany)	
Ember NR 5068	In The Beginning With Jimi Hendrix (UK)	1973
Music Distributor Q10 50082	Jimi Hendrix	1976
Soul SR1012	Jimi Hendrix (Mexico)	1982
Disques Esperance	Jimi Hendrix (France)	1975
Hor Zu SHZE 293	Jimi Hendrix Live	1972
	Jimi Hendrix Live In New Jersey	1974
Starline KS521	Jimmy Hendrix	
Astan 201016	Last Night (Germany)	1981
Strand 6.28530 (LC5830)	Legends Of Rock (Holland)	1986
	Live In New York	
Stateside 062-91630	Live, Volume 1 (France)	1984
Stateside 062-91631	Live, Volume 2 (France)	1984
Ember 3428	Looking Back With Jimi (UK)	1974
Astan 201019	Mr Pitiful (Germany)	1981
Astan 201017	My Best Friend (Germany)	1981
Astan 201018	Second Time Around (Germany)	1981
Festival 351	Still With Us (Europe)	1974
London 195 005	Strange Things (France)	1968
London SH 8369	Strange Things (UK)	1968
Showcase SHLP 101	Strange Things	1985
Interdisc ILPS 181	That Special Sound (Europe)	1968
Interdisc	The Cream Of Jimi (Europe)	1967
Baron 105	The Early Years	1972
London 379 008	The Great Jimi Hendrix In New York (Holland)	1968
Object OR 0071	The Jimi Hendrix Collection	1990
Remember 75003	The Psychedelic Voodoo Chile	1990
Strand	The Legend Of Rock: Jimi Hendrix (Holland)	1981
Hallmark SHM791	The Wild One	1973
Astan 201020	Welcome Home (Germany)	1981
MFP 5278	What'd I Say (UK)	1972
Pink Elephant	1967 Material	1976
Bigtime 2615252	16 Greatest Classics	1988
Bulldog BDL 2010	20 Golden Pieces Of Jimi Hendrix (UK)	1980

Jimi Hendrix—Little Richard Collaborations

Produced by Little Richard and Bumps Blackwell (personnel: Little Richard (v,p), Jimi Hendrix (g), Dewey Terry (g), Glen Willings (g), Don Harris (b), Henry Oden (b), others unknown) in sessions from December 1964 through June 1965. The album listed are cross-referenced with information in 'The Life and Times of Little Richard' by Charles White. (Note: According to archivist Caesar Glebbeek, 'Jimi, calling himself Maurice James, only performed and recorded with Little Richard between January 1965 to July 1965.' Thus, this claim prevents the inclusion of Hendrix on the albums 'Little Richard Is Back', 'Together' and 'Friends From The Beginning'.

VJ 1107	Little Richard Is Back	1964
VJ 1124	Little Richard's Greatest Hits	1964
Modern 1000	The Incredible Little Richard Sings His Greatest Hits—Live!	166
Modern 1030	the Wild & Frantic Little Richard	1966
Joy 195	Mr Big (UK)	1971
ALA 1972	Friends From The Beginning	1972
Joy 260	Rip It Up (UK)	1973
Dynasty 7304	Talking 'Bout Soul	1973
LSM 3001	Good Old Rock 'n Roll	1980
Everest	Jimi Hendrix-Little Richard: Roots Of Rock	1974
Joy 195	Mr Big	1971
Pickwick	Together	1974

Jimi Hendrix—Lonnie Youngblood Collaborations

Produced by Johnny Brantley (personnel: Lee Moses (b), Herman Hitson (g), Jimi Hendrix (g), Lonnie Youngblood (s))

Note: In May 1986 a US District Court found that some of the Lonnie Youngblood albums which have been released contained material that had been doctored. The claim made is that Youngblood's vocals were removed and tracks of a Hendrix imitator were added on both guitar and vocals. The court ordered those albums removed from sale, and further distribution of such discontinued. These albums includes those on the Audio Fidelity, Accord and Trip labels in the United States. (* indicates legitimate albums believed to contain unaltered material.)

Fontana 9294900	Attention (Germany)	1974
Accord SN 7101	Before London	1980
Accord SN7139	Cosmic Feeling	1981
Nutmeg NUT1002	Cosmic Turnaround	1981
Pulsar PUL 004	Experiences	1991
Byg 529912	Faces and Places (UK)	
51 West Q160 28	Flashback	1974
DJM MD 8011 (28011)	For Real (UK) *	1975
Thunderbird TDR-300	Free Spirit	1972
Accord SN 7112	Free Spirit	1981
Thunderbolt 094	Free Spirit	1990
Richmond N5-2153	From This Day On	
Topline TOP124	Gangster Of Love	1985
Trip TLP9522	Genius Of Jimi Hendrix *	1974
Festival 204	Genius of Jimi Hendrix	1978
Audio Fidelity AFEH 1027	Genius Of Jimi	1982
Intercord	Good Times (Germany)	
Musidisc 30 CV 1337/1354/1331/1315	Greatest Original Sessions*	1974
TVP	Hendrix	1977
Enterprise ENTB 1030	Hendrix 66	1972
Up	Hendrix & Youngblood (Italy)	
Shout SLP502	In The Beginning	1972
Pickwick International	Jimi	1975
Springboard SP4010	Jimi Hendrix	1974
Joker SM 3845-2	Jimi Hendrix At His Best (Italy)	1984
Signal 88110	Jimi Hendrix Experience	1991
Springboard 4031	Jimi Hendrix In Concert	1982
Enterprise ENTF 3001	Jimi Hendrix In Session	1973
Valentine SU1020	Jimi Hendrix—Superstar (Italy)	1984
Valentine SU1036	Jimi Hendrix—Superstar (Italy)	1984
Wisepack LE 603)	Jimi Hendrix, Volume 1 & 2	1992
Audio Fidelity	Jimi Hendrix, Vol 1-3	
Joker 3254	Jimi Hendrix, Vol 4 (Italy)	1984
Joker MC3536	Jimi Hendrix, Vol 5 (Italy)	
Monkey	Jimmy Hendrix (France)	
Nutmeg NUT1003	Kaleidoscope	1982
Armando ACE31	La Grande Storia Del Rock: Jimi Hendrix (#31)	1982
Armando ACE8	La Grande Storia Del Rock: Jimi Hendrix (#8)	1982
Armando ACE60	La Grande Storia Del Rock: Jimi Hendrix (#60)	1982
Armando ACE39	La Grande Storia Del Rock: Jimi Hendrix (#39)	1982
Armando ACE56	La Grande Storia Del Rock: Jimi Hendrix (#56)	1982
Armando ACE92	La Grande Storia Del Rock: Jimi Hendrix (#92)	1982
Pulsar 008	Masterpieces	1992

Trip TLP 9512	Moods	1973	London Wavelength	#542 Best Of The BBC Rock Hour	1984 (Oct 14)
Thunderbolt 075	Nightlife (Japan)	1990	Reprise PRO 4541	Between The Lines—	1990
Kaleidoscope 19026	Original Hits			The Jimi Hendrix Story	
	Prologue	1991	On The Radio 1989	Born In The USA	1989
Amer. Tape 1167C	Psycho	1977	Rolling Stone RSMP 82-24	Continuous History of Rock and Roll	1982 (March 20-21)
Trip TLP9500	Rare Hendrix	1972	Crawdaddy 5-1975	Crawdaddy Radio Revue	1969
Enterprise 3000	Rare Hendrix *	1974	22/12/86 DIR	DIR Christmas Special	1986
Musidisc 30 CV 1337	Rock Guitar (France)	1973	Radio Today	Flashback Series	1988
Springboard SPB 4042	Rock Guitar Greats	1974	MediaAmerica	Inside The Experience	1990
Trip TLP 9501	Roots Of Hendrix	1972	U.S. Army USA-IS 67-A	In Sound	1967 (October)
Musidisc 1354	Super Hendrix		AFRTS RL-7-4	Jimi Hendrix	1974
Napolean	That Unforgettable Jimi Hendrix (Italy)		BBC LP37480	Jimi Hendrix	1976
United Artists LA 505	The Very Best Of Jimi Hendrix (UK)	1975	The Source NBC 82-41	Jimi Hendrix: A Tribute	1982
Maple LPM6004	Two Great Experiences Together *	1971	Westwood One	Jimi Hendrix: Live & Unreleased	1988 (September)
Trip 1622	16 Greatest Hits (Great Songs)	1976	Castle HB100	Jimi Hendrix: Live & Unreleased	1989
			Metal Shop	Metalshop Radio	1984
Jimi Hendrix Radio Shows			American Forces Radio & Television	Midnight Landing	1975
			Service P-15693	Raised On Radio	1988
Reprise PRO-A-840	And A Happy New Year	1979	On The Radio	Rarities, Vol 1	1990
	(Christmas medley)		On The Radio	Rarities, Vol 3	1991
Arm Forces Radio Series RL-7-4	American Forces Army Radio Show	1984	Westwood One 081384	Rock And Roll Never Forgets	1984 (Aug 13)
MediaAmerica	At The Core-Rock From The Inside:	1989	Rock Scope	Rock Scope	1981
	Beginnings		Media America	Setting The Record Straight	1992
	BBC Classic Tracks: 16/12/91	1991	ABC Rock Radio	The Official History Of Rock 'n' Roll	1989
	BBC Classic Tracks: 6/1/92	1992	Schoeder Intl	75 Hits From Our Catalogue	1969
	BBC Classic Tracks: 23/3/92	1992	BBC	60's At The Beeb	1986

Singles and EPs Released/Produced by Jimi Hendrix and Experience Members

(b)=bassist (d)=drummer (g)=guitarist (p)=pianist (v)=vocalist

Accidental Love / Nothing Can Change This Love
    artist: Loving Kind, Noel Redding (b). Piccadilly/Pye 7N 35299. released: 1966.

Ain't That Peculiar / Rhyme and Reason
    artist: Loving Kind, Noel Redding (b). Piccadilly/Pye 7N 35342. released: 1966.

All Along The Watchtower / Burning Of The Midnight Lamp
    artist: Jimi Hendrix Experience, Noel Redding (b), Mitch Mitchell (d). Reprise 0767. released: 9/68. Billboard charted 9/21/68 climbing to #20. Entered Cashbox charts 9/14/68, taking seven weeks to climb to #18, lasting a total of 10 weeks on the charts.

All Along The Watchtower / All Along The Watchtower
    artists: Jimi Hendrix Experience, Noel Redding (b), Mitch Mitchell (d). Reprise 0293 radio promo.

All Along The Watchtower / Voodoo Chile
    artist: Jimi Hendrix Experience, Noel Redding (b), Mitch Mitchell (d). Polydor (Germany) 210012, Barclay (France) 61 381. released: 1972.

All Along The Watchtower / Can You See Me
    artist: Jimi Hendrix Experience, Noel Redding (b), Mitch Mitchell (d). Polydor (Germany) 59 240, Polydor RTB 53530 (Yugoslavia), Polydor 60041 (Spain).

All Along The Watchtower / Crosstown Traffic
    artist: Jimi Hendrix Experience, Noel Redding (b), Mitch Mitchell (d). Reprise GRE 0742. Reissued in their 'Back To Back' greatest hits series.

All Along The Watchtower / Foxy Lady / Purple Haze / Manic Depression
    artist: Jimi Hendrix Experience, Noel Redding (b), Mitch Mitchell (d). Polydor (UK) POSPX 401. released: 12/81.

All Along The Watchtower / Gloria
    artist: Jimi Hendrix. Polydor (Australia) 2141 120.

All Along The Watchtower / Hey Joe / Purple Haze / The Wind Cries Mary
    artist: Jimi Hendrix Experience, Noel Redding (b), Mitch Mitchell (d). Polydor (Germany) 2607-001.

All Along The Watchtower / Hey Joe / The Wind Cries Mary
    artist: Jimi Hendrix Experience, Noel Redding (b), Mitch Mitchell (d). Polydor (Holland) 2200 135.

All Along The Watchtower / Hey Joe / Voodoo Chile
    artist: Jimi Hendrix Experience, Noel Redding (b), Mitch Mitchell (d). Track (UK) 2095-001, Polydor 2121 011 (Germany). released: 1969.

All Along The Watchtower / Long Hot Summer Night
    artist: Jimi Hendrix Experience, Noel Redding (b), Mitch Mitchell (d). Track (UK) 604 025, Polydor (UK) 2141 278, Barclay (France) 60993. released: 10/68. Reissued in UK 9/80 on Polydor 2141 278.

All Along The Watchtower / Foxy Lady
    artist: Jimi Hendrix Experience, Noel Redding (b), Mitch Mitchell (d). Old Gold (UK) 9432.

All Along The Watchtower / Hey Joe
    artist: Jimi Hendrix Experience, Noel Redding (b), Mitch Mitchell (d). Polydor 213 5001 (Germany). Part of German 'Golden Greats' Series.

All I Want / Segue III
    artist: Lonnie Youngblood, Jimi Hendrix (g), Lee Moses (b), Herman Hitson (g), Lonnie Youngblood (s). Cobra (Italy) B004.

All I Want / Groovemaker / Sweat Thang / Goodbye Bessie Mae
    artist: Lonnie Youngblood, Jimi Hendrix (g), Lee Moses (b), Herman Hitson (g), Lonnie Youngblood (s). Musidisc (France) V1348.

Angel / Night Bird Flying
    artist: Jimi Hendrix Experience, Noel Redding (b), Mitch Mitchell (d). Track 2094 007. released: 4/71.

Angel / Freedom
    artist: Jimi Hendrix Experience, Billy Cox (b), Mitch Mitchell (d). Polydor (Germany) 2120 040, Polydor (Italy) 2121 040.

Auld Lang Syne / The Little Drummer Boy / Silent Night
    artist: Band Of Gypsys, Jimi Hendrix (g), Billy Cox (b), Buddy Miles (d). Reprise PRO-A-840. released: 1974. First released as a radio station-only promotional album by Reprise in 1974. Later released as 12" 33-rpm EP in 1979, and as a 7" 45-rpm picture disc in 1980.

Baby What You Want Me To Do I & II
    artist: Little Richard, Jimi Hendrix (g), Little Richard (p). Modern 1043. released: 1966. According to Little Richard, Hendrix played on some of the Modern recordings, including this one, in his biography by Charles White.

Ballad Of Jimi / Gloomy Monday
    artist: Curtis Knight, Jimi Hendrix (g), Curtis Knight (g), Bernard Purdie or Ray Lucas (d), Marvin Held (b). London (UK) HL 10321, King Top (Japan) 1570, Decca (Holland) 25430. released: 10/70.

Ballad Of Jimi / Sugar And Spice
    artist: Curtis Knight, Jimi Hendrix (g), Curtis Knight (g,v), Bernard Purdie or Ray Lucas (d), Marvin Held (d). Stateside (France) 2C006 91963.

Beginnings
    artist: Jimi Hendrix. Guitar Player 7375XS. released: 9/75. Flexi-disc included in Guitar Player magazine special Jimi Hendrix issue.

Blue Suede Shoes / Johnny B. Goode
    artist: Jimi Hendrix. Barclay (France) 61 550. released: 1972. Part of the 'Jimi Hendrix Story—Vol 1-12' series.

Burning Of The Midnight Lamp / The Stars That Play With Laughing Sam's Dice
    artist: Jimi Hendrix Experience, Noel Redding (b), Mitch Mitchell (d). Track (UK) 604 007, Barclay (France) 60 858, Polydor (Germany) 59 117, Polydor (Sweden) 59 117. released: 8/67. Reissued in UK 9/80 on Polydor 2141 278.

California Night / Get Out Of My Life Woman
    artist: Jimi Hendrix, Curtis Knight (g,v), Bernard Purdie or Ray Lucas (d), Marvin Held (b). label unknown (Yugoslavia), Stateside (Italy) 3C006 92352.

Can You Dance To It / Marie
    artist: Cat Mother And The All Night Newsboys. Polydor PD-14407. Produced by Jimi Hendrix.

Can You See Me / Crosstown Traffic / Foxy Lady / Hey Joe
    artist: Jimi Hendrix Experience, Noel Redding (b), Mitch Mitchell (d). Visadisc (France) VI 295. released: 1968.

Changes / Message Of Love
    artist: Jimi Hendrix, Buddy Miles (d), Billy Cox (b). Barclay (France) 61 362. released: 1972. Part of the 'Jimi Hendrix Story—Vol 1-12' series.

Above: This photo montage conveys only a fraction of the excitement Jimi created in performance.

Left: Released a year after Hendrix's death, *Rainbow Bridge* featured recordings from a live performance Jimi made atop the volcano Haleakala on the Hawaiian Island of Maui on 30 July 1970.

Right: Hendrix appealed to heaven's invisible justice against Earth's visible force. He knew that it—the invisible—is strong and alone. He was a believer in the truth of things, a *seer* seeing through the show of things. If he had not first been a prophet, he would never have been such a great performer.

Changing Days / Whiskey Place
artist: Ramatam (Mitch Mitchell). Atlantic/Pioneer (Japan) P1169A. released: 10/72.

Come On / 1983
artist: Jimi Hendrix, Noel Redding (b), Mitch Mitchell (d). Barclay 61 396. released: 1972. Part of the 'Jimi Hendrix Story—Vol 1-12' series.

Crosstown Traffic / (Crossroads)
artist: Jimi Hendrix Experience, Noel Redding (b), Mitch Mitchell (d). Polydor AS 046 (Italy). Italian jukebox record. B-side features 'Crossroads' by Cream.

Crosstown Traffic / Voodoo Chile (Slight Return)
artist: Jimi Hendrix, Noel Redding (b), Mitch Mitchell (d). Polydor 873 855. released: 1990. Released in conjunction with Wrangler Jeans European TV campaign using 'Crosstown Traffic' as music bed.

Crosstown Traffic / Voodoo Chile (Slight Return) / All Along The Watchtower / Have You Ever Been (To Electric Ladyland)
artist: Jimi Hendrix, Noel Redding (b), Mitch Mitchell (d). Polydor 940. released: 1990. Released as 12'-EP and CD in conjunction with Wrangler Jeans European TV campaign using 'Crosstown Traffic' as music bed.

Crosstown Traffic / Fire / Foxy Lady / Remember / Little Miss Strange / May This Be Love
artist: Jimi Hendrix Experience, Noel Redding (b), Mitch Mitchell (d). Polydor Club Selektion (Germany) 2835 040. released: 1968.

Crosstown Traffic / Gypsy Eyes
artist: Jimi Hendrix Experience, Noel Redding (b), Mitch Mitchell (d). Reprise 0792, Polydor (Germany) 59256, Track (UK) 604 029, Barclay (France) 061 038/061 361, Ariola (Spain) 14.925. released: 11/68. Billboard charted 30/11/68 climbing to #52. Entered Cashbox charts 11/30/68, taking five weeks to climb to #36, dropping off after eight weeks. Released in Europe 4/69 on Track (UK) and Barclay (France). Part of the 'Jimi Hendrix Story—Vol 1-12' series.

Daytripper / Hush Now
artist: Curtis Knight, Jimi Hendrix (g), Curtis Knight (g,v), Bernard Purdie or Ray Lucas (d), Marvin Held (b). Visadisc (France) JLR 3.

Dolly Dagger / Dolly Dagger
artist: Jimi Hendrix, Billy Cox (b), Buddy Miles (d). Reprise 1044. released: 10/71. Stereo/mono two-sided promo single.

Dolly Dagger / Star Spangled Banner
artist: Jimi Hendrix, Billy Cox (b), Buddy Miles (d). Reprise 1044. released: 10/71. Billboard charted 23/10/71 climbing to #74. Hit Cashbox charts 30/10/71 at #93, dropping to #100 the next week and falling off. Released as two-sided single in stereo and mono.

Do You Feel It I & II
artist: Little Richard, Jimi Hendrix (g), Little Richard (p). Modern 1019. released: June, 1966. According to Little Richard, Hendrix played on some of the Modern recordings, including this one, in his biography by Charles White.

Doriella de Fontaine / Doriella de Fontaine (instrumental)
artist: Jimi Hendrix, Lightnin' Rod (v), Buddy Miles (d). Celluloid 106, Carrere (UK) 332. released: 1984

Drifting / Ezy Rider
artist: Jimi Hendrix. Barclay (France) 61 428. released: 1972. Part of the 'Jimi Hendrix Story—Vol 1-12' series.

Everlasting First / Keep On Shining
artist: Love, Jimi Hendrix (g), Arthur Lee (g). King (Japan) HIT-1839. released: 1/71.

Fire
artist: Jimi Hendrix Experience, Noel Redding (b), Mitch Mitchell (d). Polydor AS 076 (Italy). Italian jukebox single.

Fire / Burning Of The Midnight Lamp
artist: Jimi Hendrix Experience, Noel Redding (b), Mitch Mitchell (d). Track (UK) 604 033, Polydor (Germany) 59375, Polydor (Yugoslavia) RTB 553579, Polydor (Spain) 6079. released: 10/69.

Fire / Are You Experienced
artist: Jimi Hendrix Experience, Noel Redding (b), Mitch Mitchell (d). CBS (UK) 132 749, Mediamotion (Germany) 600 583. released: 1982. Released in conjunction with 'Jimi Hendrix Concerts' album.

Fire / Highway Child / Purple Haze / The Wind Cries Mary
artist: Jimi Hendrix, Noel Redding (b), Mitch Mitchell (d). Barclay (France) 71 157. released: 1967.

Fire / Little Wing
artist: Jimi Hendrix Experience, Noel Redding (b), Mitch Mitchell (d). Reprise 7-29845. released: 1982. From the 'Jimi Hendrix Concerts' album.

Foxy Lady / Bold As Love
artist: Jimi Hendrix Experience, Noel Redding (b), Mitch Mitchell (d). Barclay (France) 60 902. released: 1967. Released as a jukebox single.

Foxy Lady / Hey Joe
artist: Jimi Hendrix, Noel Redding (b), Mitch Mitchell (d). Reprise 0641. released: 11/67. Billboard charted 12/23/67 climbing to #67. Hit Cashbox charts 30/12/67 for three weeks positioned at #91, #83, #85.

Foxy Lady / Manic Depression
artist: Jimi Hendrix Experience, Noel Redding (b), Mitch Mitchell (d). Polydor (Italy) 59159.

Foxy Lady / Purple Haze
artist: Jimi Hendrix Experience, Noel Redding (b), Mitch Mitchell (d). Reprise 0728, Reprise (US) GRE 0728. released: 1968. Reissued 1983 by Reprise in their 'Back To Back' greatest hits series.

Foxy Lady / Spanish Castle Magic
artist: Jimi Hendrix Experience, Noel Redding (b), Mitch Mitchell (d). Polydor (Japan).

Freedom / Freedom
artist: Jimi Hendrix, Billy Cox (b), Mitch Mitchell (d). Reprise 1000. released: 4/71. Stereo/mono two-sided promo single.

Freedom / Angel
artist: Jimi Hendrix, Jimi Hendrix (g), Billy Cox (b), Mitch Mitchell (d). Reprise 1000, Polydor (Germany) 2121 040, Polydor (Italy) 2121 040. released: 4/71. Billboard charted 3/4/71 climbing to #59. Cashbox charted 2/3/71, climbing to #76, spending a total of six weeks on the chart.

Gloria
artist: Jimi Hendrix Experience, Noel Redding (b), Mitch Mitchell (d). Reprise JIMI 1. released: 1978. First released as bonus record with the albums 'The Essential Jimi Hendrix' (Reprise JIMI-1, Polydor UK KI4012). Later released in England as a 12'-EP (Polydor 2141 120). Also released in Italy (Polydor JIMI-1).

Good Old Rock & Roll / Bad News
artist: Cat Mother And The All Night Newsboys. Polydor (UK) PD-14002, Polydor (Japan) DP1659. released: 12/69. Produced by Jimi Hendrix.

Gypsy Eyes / Hey Joe / Voodoo Chile / Third Stone From The Sun
artist: Jimi Hendrix Experience, Noel Redding (b), Mitch Mitchell (d). Polydor (UK) POS PX608. released: 1981.

Gypsy Eyes / Remember / Purple Haze / Stone Free
artist: Jimi Hendrix Experience, Noel Redding (b), Mitch Mitchell (d). Track 2094 010. released: 10/71.

Hear My Train / Rock Me Baby
artist: Jimi Hendrix Experience, Noel Redding (b), Mitch Mitchell (d). Reprise K 14286. released: 1973.

Hey Joe / All Along The Watchtower
artist: Jimi Hendrix Experience, Noel Redding (b), Mitch Mitchell (d). Polydor (Germany) 2135 001.

Hey Joe
artist: Jimi Hendrix Experience, Noel Redding (b), Mitch Mitchell (d). Poster Press (UK). Flexi-disc which appeared in Melody Maker magazine.

Hey Joe / Purple Haze / The Wind Cries Mary / All Along The Watchtower
artist: Jimi Hendrix Experience, Noel Redding (b), Mitch Mitchell (d). Polydor (Germany) 2607 001.

Hey Joe / Stone Free / 51st Anniversary / Can You See Me
artist: Jimi Hendrix Experience, Noel Redding (b), Mitch Mitchell (d). Barclay (France) 071 111, Ariola (Spain).

Hey Joe / Burning Of The Midnight Lamp / May This Be Love / Highway Child
artist: Jimi hendrix Experience, Noel Redding (b), Mitch Mitchell (d). Mini Bonus 5' EP.

Hey Joe / Stone Free
artist: Jimi Hendrix Experience, Noel Redding (b), Mitch Mitchell (d). Polydor (UK) 56139, Polydor (Germany) 59 061, Polydor (UK) 2141 275, Polydor (France) 59 061, Polydor (Japan), Old Gold (UK) 9429, Polydor (Sweden) 59 061. released: 12/66. Reissued in UK 9/80 on Polydor 2141 275.

Hey Joe / Stone Free Purple Haze / 51st Anniversary The Wind Cries Mary / Highway Chile The Burning Of The Midnight Lamp / The Stars That Play With Laughing Sam's Dice All Along The Watchtower /

Long Hot Summer Night Voodoo Chile / Gloria
artist: Jimi Hendrix Experience, Noel Redding (b), Mitch Mitchell (d). Polydor 260 8001. released: 9/80. Six singles released in box set.

Hey Joe / Purple Haze
artist: Jimi Hendrix, Noel Redding (b), Mitch Mitchell (d). Polydor (Yugoslavia) 2001 993, Polydor (Europe) 53847.

Hey Joe / 51st Anniversary
artist: Jimi Hendrix Experience, Noel Redding (b), Mitch Mitchell (d). Reprise 0572. released: 5/67.

Hornet's Nest
artist: Curtis Knight, Jimi Hendrix (g). RSVP.

Hot Trigger / Good Feeling
artist: Jimi Hendrix, Lonnie Youngblood (s), Herman Hitson (g), Lee Moses (b). Explosive (France) 128 017.

Hot Trigger / Suspicious
artist: Jimi Hendrix, Lonnie Youngblood (s), Jimi Hendrix (g), Herman Hitson (g), Lee Moses (b). Trip TX 3002.

How Would You Feel / You Don't Want Me
artist: Curtis Knight, Jimi Hendrix (g), Curtis Knight (g), Bernard Purdie or Ray Lucas (d), Marvin Held (b). Track (UK) 604 009, Decca (Germany) 019 888, Decca (France) D19 888, King (Japan) TOP 1570. released: 9/67 (originally).

Hush Now / Flashing
artist: Curtis Knight, Jimi Hendrix (g), Curtis Knight (g), Bernard Purdie or Ray Lucas (d), Marvin Held (b). London (UK) HL 10160, London (Germany) 20850, London (France) 69 002. released: 10/67.

Hush Now / Love Love
artist: Curtis Knight, Jimi Hendrix (g), Curtis Knight (g,v), Bernard Purdie or Ray Lucas (d), Marvin Held (b). Ariola 14925 (Spain).

I Don't Know What You've Got, Part 1 & 2
artist: Little Richard, Jimi Hendrix (g), Little Richard (p), Dewey Terry (g), Glen Willing (g), Don Harris (b). Vee Jay 698. released: 1965. Billboard charted 11/27/65 climbing to #92.

I Love The Things You Do / Treat Me Nice
artist: Loving Kind, Noel Redding (b). Piccadilly/Pye 7N 35318. released: 1966.

I'm A Man / Bright Lights, Big City
artist: Jimi Hendrix, Curtis Knight (g), Bernard Purdie or Ray Lucas (d), Marvin Held (b). EMI-Stateside (Germany) 006-91709.

I'm A Man / Bright Lights, Big City / No Such Animal, Part 1 / No Such Animal, Part 2
    artist: Jimi Hendrix, Curtis Knight (g), Bernard Purdie or Ray Lucas (d), Marvin Held (b). Blue Flame 5205. Label lists artist as 'Jimmy James and the Blue Flames.'

Izabella / Star Spangled Banner
    artist: Jimi Hendrix. Barclay (France) 61 487. released: 1972. Released as part of the 'Jimi Hendrix Story, Vol 1-12.'

Johnny B. Goode / Little Wing
    artist: Jimi Hendrix Experience, Noel Redding (b), Mitch Mitchell (d). Polydor 2001 277. released: 1/72.

Johnny B. Goode / Johnny B. Goode
    artist: Jimi Hendrix, Noel Redding (b), Mitch Mitchell (d). Reprise 1082 (US), Polydor AS 139 (Italy). released: 1983. Stereo/mono two-sided promo single. Released in Italy as jukebox single.

Johnny B. Goode / Lover Man
    artist: Jimi Hendrix, Noel Redding (b), Mitch Mitchell (d). Reprise 1082. released: 1983. Released in conjunction with Jimi Hendrix Concerts album.

Little Wing / (Johnny Reggae)
    artist: Jimi Hendrix, Noel Redding (b), Mitch Mitchell (d). Polydor AS 132 (Italy). Italian jukebox single. B-side 'Johnny Reggae' by the Piglets.

Looking For A Love / The Last Girl
    artist: Isley Brothers, Jimi Hendrix (g). Atlantic 2263.

Magic Forest / Bright New Day
    artist: Fat Mattress (Noel Redding). Polydor (Japan) DP 1695. released: 5/70.

May This Be Love / 51st Anniversary
    artist: Jimi Hendrix, Noel Redding (b), Mitch Mitchell (d). Barclay (France) 61 389. released: 1972. Released as part of the 'Jimi Hendrix Story, Vol 1-12.'

Move Over And Let Me Dance / Have You Ever Been Disappointed
    artist: Isley Brothers, Jimi Hendrix (g). Atlantic 2303.

My Diary / Utee
    artist: Rosa Lee Brooks, Jimi Hendrix (g), Arthur Lee (g), Rosa Lee Brooks (v). Revis. released: 1963. First known pressed recording of Jimi Hendrix.

Naturally / Irridescent Butterfly
    artist: Fat Mattress, Noel Redding (b). Polydor (UK) 56352, Polydor (Japan) DP 1673. released: 1969.

No Such Animal, Parts 1 & 2 / Soul Food / Goodbye Bessie Mae / Go Go Shoes / My Diary / Utee
    artist: Jimi Hendrix, Lonnie Youngblood, Rosa Lee Brooks. Rock Legend RWJH-07. released: 1987.

No Such Animal, Part 1 / No Such Animal, Part II
    artist: Curtis Knight, Curtis Knight (g), Bernard Purdie or Ray Lucas (d), Marvin Held (b). Audio Fidelity 167, Bellaphon (Germany) 18019, Columbia (Japan) LL-2423-AF released: 1970.

One Rainy Wish / Up From The Skies
    artist: Jimi Hendrix Experience, Noel Redding (b), Mitch Mitchell (d). Reprise 0665, Barclay (France) 60 959, Polydor (Spain) 60025. released: 1967.

Opening Jam / C' Blues
    artist: Jimi Hendrix, Noel Redding (b), Mitch Mitchell (d). Vogue (France) 4006. released: 1971.

Opening Jam / Smashing Of Amps
    artist: Jimi Hendrix, Noel Redding (b), Mitch Mitchell (d). Ari (Germany) 14937.

Purple Haze / Stone Free / Gypsy Eyes / Remember
    artist: Jimi Hendrix Experience, Noel Redding (b), Mitch Mitchell (d). Track (UK) 2094 010.

Purple Haze / The Wind Cries Mary
    artist: Jimi Hendrix Experience, Noel Redding (b), Mitch Mitchell (d). Reprise 0597, Old Gold (UK) 9430, Barclay (France) 71157. released: 6/67. Billboard charted 8/26/67 climbing to #65. Entered Cashbox charts 9/2/67, taking five weeks to climb to #64, spending a total of nine weeks on the charts.

Purple Haze / 51st Anniversary
    artist: Jimi Hendrix Experience, Noel Redding (b), Mitch Mitchell (d). Track (UK) 604 001, Polydor (Japan) DPQ 6912, Polydor (Germany) 59072, Polydor (UK) 2141 276. released: 3/67. Reissued in UK 9/80 on Polydor 2141 276.

Purple Haze / Highway Chile
    artist: Jimi Hendrix Experience, Noel Redding (b), Mitch Mitchell (d). Barclay (France) 61 359, Napolean (Italy) NP 1018.

Red House / The Wind Cries Mary
    artist: Jimi Hendrix, Noel Redding (b), Mitch Mitchell (d). Barclay (France) 61 360. released: 1972. Released as part of the 'Jimi Hendrix Story, Vol 1-12.'

Red House / Spanish Castle Magic
    artist: Jimi Hendrix Experience, Noel Redding (b), Mitch Mitchell (d). Polydor (UK). released: 1967. Rolling Stone flexi-disc.

Rock 'n' Roll Band / Yes I Need Someone
    artist: Eire Apparent, Eire Apparent. Buddah 201 039, Polydor. released: 1969. Hendrix sat is as guest artist with Eire Apparent for an album he also produced.

Slippin' and Slidin'
    artist: Little Richard. Modern 1030. released: 1966. Little Richard claims Hendrix may have played on this track during a 1965 session.

Simon Says / Wild As A Tiger
    artist: Isley Brothers, Jimi Hendrix (g). Atlantic 2277.

Soul Food / Bessie Mae
    artist: Lonnie Youngblood, Jimi Hendrix (g), Lonnie Youngblood (s). Fairmount.

Spanish Castle Magic / Fire / Hey Joe
    artist: Jimi Hendrix Experience, Noel Redding (b), Mitch Mitchell (d). blank. released: 1982. Three-song 7" 33-rpm EP of live Stockholm show.

Stepping Stone / Izabella
    artist: Band Of Gypsys, Jimi Hendrix (g), Billy Cox (b), Buddy Miles (d). Reprise 0905. released: 1970.

Stepping Stone / Tax Free
    artist: Jimi Hendrix. Barclay (France) 61 660. released: 1972. Released as part of the 'Jimi Hendrix Story, Vol 1-12.'

Stone Free / If Six Was Nine
    artist: Jimi Hendrix Experience, Noel Redding (b), Mitch Mitchell (d). Reprise 0853. released: 1969.

Testify, Part 1 / Testify, Part 2
    artist: Isley Brothers, Jimi Hendrix (g). T-Neck 501. released: 1964. This record was released in two different versions. The promo copy featured 'Testify, Part 1' and 'Testify, Part 2' (take 3). The commercial release contained 'Testify, Part 1' (take 4) and 'Testify, Part 2.'

The Everlasting First / Keep On Shining
    artist: Love, Jimi Hendrix (g). Blue Thumb 7116. Jimi Hendrix played guitar on 'The Everlasting First.'

The Grass Will Sing For You / Wooly Bully
    artist: Lonnie Youngblood, Jimi Hendrix (g). Fairmount F-1016.

The Wind Cries Mary / Highway Child
    artist: Jimi Hendrix Experience, Noel Redding (b), Mitch Mitchell (d). Track (UK) 604 004, Polydor (Germany) 59 078, Barclay (France) 61 360, Barclay (France) 60 840 (promo), Polydor (Sweden) 59 078. released: 5/67. Reissued in UK 9/80 on Polydor 2141 277.

The Wind Cries Mary / Red House
    artist: Jimi Hendrix Experience, Noel Redding (b), Mitch Mitchell (d). Barclay (France) 61 360.

The Wind Cries Mary / Voodoo Chile
    artist: Jimi Hendrix Experience, Noel Redding (b), Mitch Mitchell (d). Polydor 213 5013 (Germany). Part of German 'Golden Greats' Series.

The Wind Cries Mary / The Wind Cries Mary
    artist: Jimi Hendrix Experience, Noel Redding (b), Mitch Mitchell (d). Reprise 1118. Released as two-sided stereo/mono promo single.

The Wind Cries Mary / Little Wing
    artist: Jimi Hendrix Experience, Noel Redding (b), Mitch Mitchell (d). Reprise 1118. Commercial release.

Up From The Skies / One Rainy Wish
    artist: Jimi Hendrix Experience, Noel Redding (b), Mitch Mitchell (d). Reprise 0665. released: 1968. Billboard charted 3/16/68 climbing to #82.

Voodoo Chile / All Along The Watchtower
    artist: Jimi Hendrix Experience, Noel Redding (b), Mitch Mitchell (d). Polydor (Germany) 2121 012.

Voodoo Chile / Gloria
    artist: Jimi Hendrix Experience, Noel Redding (b), Mitch Mitchell (d). Polydor 2141 280, Polydor (France) 2141 280. released: 9/80. Part of reissue package in UK 9/80.

Voodoo Chile / Hey Joe / All Along The Watchtower
    artist: Jimi Hendrix Experience, Noel Redding (b), Mitch Mitchell (d). Track (UK) 2095 001. released: 10/70.

Waterfall / 51st Anniversary
    artist: Jimi Hendrix Experience, Noel Redding (b), Mitch Mitchell (d). Barclay (France) 61389.

Whole Lotta Shakin' / Goodnight Irene
    artist: Little Richard, Jimi Hendrix (g), Little Richard (p), Dewey Terry (g), Glen Willing (g), Don Harris (b). Vee Jay 612, Stateside (Italy) 60029. released: 1964. Little Richard claims Hendrix was on these sessions in his biography by Charles White.

Wipe The Sweat (Part 1 & 2)
    artist: Lonnie Youngblood, Jimi Hendrix (g), Lonnie Youngblood (s), Herman Hitson (b). Maple 1003.

Why Don't You Love Me / Goodnight Irene
    artist: Little Richard, Jimi Hendrix (g), Little Richard (p), Black Arthur (g), Henry Oden (b), Bumps Blackwell (d). Ala 1175. released: 1972. Little Richard claims Hendrix was on these sessions in his biography by Charles White. Record released to capitalize on Jimi's post-mortem popularity. 'Why Don't You Love Me' side listed only as Little Richard, while 'Goodnight Irene' listed as Little Richard and Jimi Hendrix.

Yes I Need Someone / Let Me Stay
    artist: Eire Apparent, Jimi Hendrix (g). Buddah BDA 67. Jimi Hendrix plays on 'Yes I Need Someone.'

69 Freedom Special / Miss Lady
    artist: Buddy Miles. Mercury 72903. Jimi Hendrix produced.

Note: Polydor in Europe released a set of two artist singles. Included:

Up From The Skies (Jimi Hendrix Experience) / Jumbo (Bee Gees)
    (Polydor AS 020)

Johnny B Goode (Jimi Hendrix Experience) / Inner City Blues (Impressions) (Polydor AS 139)

Jimi Hendrix Compact Discs

Acoustic Jams (Sphinx CD001—Italy)
All Along The Watchtower (Polydor 879 061-2—UK)
All Along The Watchtower (Polydor 879 583-2—France)
All The Hits (Duchesse 352061-2—Holland)
American Dream (World Productions 023—Italy)
Are You Experienced? (Reprise 6261-2—USA)
Are You Experienced? HMV box set with booklet—UK)
Are You Experienced? (Polydor P20P-22001—Japan)
Are You Experienced? (Polydor P33P-50036—Japan)
Are You Experienced? (Polydor POCP-2019—Japan)
Are You Experienced? (Polydor 825 416—Germany)
Are You Experienced? (Polydor 847 234-2—UK)
Are You Experienced? / Band Of Gypsys / In The West / War Heroes
 (Polydor 839 875-2—UK)
Atlanta Special (TGP 121—Italy)
Axis: Bold As Love (Reprise 6281-2—USA)
Axis: Bold As Love (Polydor P20P-22002—Japan)
Axis: Bold As Love (Polydor P33P-25023—Japan)
Axis: Bold As Love (Polydor POCP-2020—Japan)
Axis: Bold As Love (Polydor 847 243-2—UK)
Axis: Bold As Love—Jimi Hendrix Experience In 1967
 (UFO 1-873884-03-5—UK)
Back In Time (Teledisc sampler—UK)
Band Of Gypsys (Polydor 821 933-2—Germany)
Band Of Gypsys (Polydor 847 237-2—UK)
Band Of Gypsys (Polydor P20P-22006—Japan)
Band Of Gypsys (Polydor P33P-25022—Japan)
Band Of Gypsys (Polydor POCP-2020—Japan)
Band Of Gypsys (On Stage 12022—Italy)
Band Of Gypsys: Happy New Year (Silver Shadow 9103)
Band Of Gypsys, Vol 3 (Beech Martin—Italy)
BBC Classic Tracks: 12/16/91
BBC Classic Tracks: 1/6/92
BBC Classic Tracks: 3/23/92
Best Of & Rest Of Jimi Hendrix (Action Replay CDAR 1022—UK)
Best Of The BBC Radio One (UK)
Black Devil (Great Dane 9104—Italy)
British Beat Live In Germany 1966-67 (The Early Years 02-3303)
Broadcasts (Luna 9204—Italy)
Cafe Au-Go-Go (Koine 880802—Italy)
Calling Long Distance (Univibes UV1001—UK)
Canadian Club (World Productions 006-2—Italy)
Cherokee Mist (Silver Shadow 9103—Italy)
Cornerstones (Polydor 847 231-2—UK)
Cornerstones (Polydor POCP-1064—Japan)
Crash Landing (Polydor P33P-25024—Japan)
Crash Landing (Polydor P20P-22007—Japan)
Crash Landing (Polydor POCP-2022—Japan)
Crash Landing (Reprise 2204—USA)
Crash Landing (Polydor 837 932-2—Germany)
Crosstown Traffic (Polydor 873 855-2—UK)
Cry Of Love (Polydor P33P-25011—Japan)
Cry Of Love (Polydor P20P-22007—Japan)
Cry Of Love (Polydor POCP-2023—Japan)
Cry Of Love (Reprise 2034—USA)
Cry Of Love (Polydor 829 926-2—Germany)
Cry Of Love (Polydor 847 242-2—UK)
Daytripper (Rykodisc—RCD3-1008—USA)
Doriella du Fontaine (Restless72663-2—USA)
Early Classics (Pair SCD 4926—USA)
Electric Hendrix, Vol 1 (Pyramid 030—Italy)
Electric Hendrix, Vol 2 (Pyramid 031—Italy)
Electric Hendrix, Vol 2 aka Band Of Gypsys 2 mispressing (bootleg)
Electric Gypsys (Pilot HJCD 070—Italy)
Electric Jimi (Jaguarondi CD 001/2—Italy)
Electric Ladyland (Reprise 6307-2—USA)
Electric Ladyland (Polydor 823 359-2—Germany)
Electric Ladyland (Polydor P36P-22004/5—Japan)
Electric Ladyland (Polydor P58P 25001/2—Japan)
Electric Ladyland (Polydor POCP-2023—Japan)
Electric Ladyland (Polydor 847 233-2—UK)
Electric 70s (BB 1011—UK)
Electronic Church Music (Pyramid CD23—Italy)

Electric Hendrix 1 (Pyramid CD30—Italy)
Electric Hendrix 2 (Pyramid CD31—Italy)
Electric Jimi (Jaguarondi 001/2—Italy)
Essential Jimi Hendrix, Vol 1 & 2 (Warner 26035)
Experience (Signal 88110—Holland)
Experience (Galaxis 9006—Germany)
Experience At Royal Albert Hall (Jimco JIM 0043—Japan)
Experience In Europe '67-69 (Vulture 009/2—Italy)
Experience Soundtrack (Bulldog 40023—UK)
Experience II (MTT 10.21—Italy)
Experiences (Pulsar PUL 004—Holland)
Fire (Swingin' Pig 018)
First Rays Of The New Rising Sun (Living Legend 023—Italy)
First Time In Canada (Bunny BM 1092)
Footlights (Polydor 847 235-2—UK 4-CD box set)
Free Spirit (Magnum/Thunderbolt CDTB 094—UK)
Fuzz, Feedback & Wah Wah (Hal Leonard 00660035) *
Gimme The Glad Eye (Double Time 003—bootleg)
Gloria/Purple Haze/Hey Joe/Voodoo Chile
 (Polydor 887 585-2—Germany)
Great Hits USA (Mikasa Tsusho GH-1841—Japan)
Greatest Guitar Heroes (Polydor P22P 20073—Japan)
Guitar Hero (Document DR 013—Italy)
Guitar Heroes Collection (Teichiku TECP-25180—Japan)
Guitars And Amps (World Productions 005—Italy)
Gypsy Suns And Rainbows (Manic Depression 006—Italy)
Gypsy Suns, Moons And Rainbows (Sidewalk JHX 8868—Italy)
Hendrix Speaks (Rhino 70771)
Here It Is, The Music (Rykodisc 00099—USA)
Historic Hendrix (Pair SPCD2-1155—USA)
Historic Performances (Aquarius 8Q67-JH-080)
I Don't Live Today (Living Legend 030—Italy)
In Concert (Starlife 36121—UK)
In The West (Polydor P33P-25004—Japan)
In The West (Polydor P20P-22009—Japan)
In The West (Polydor 831 312-2—Germany)
Incident At Rainbow Bridge/Isle Of Wight
 (Pyramid PYCD 060-2—Italy)
Introspective (Tabak CINT 5006—UK)
Island Man (Silver Rarities SIRA 039/40—Italy)
Isle Of Wight (Polydor P33P-25010—Japan)
Isle Of Wight (Polydor P20P-22008—Japan)
Isle Of Wight (Polydor POCP-2028—Japan)
Isle Of Wight (Polydor 831 312-2—Germany)
Isle Of Wight (Polydor 847 236-2—UK)
Isle Of Wight (Polydor—UK (Footlights))
It Never Takes An End: Newport Pop (TGP 118—Italy)
Jimi Hendrix (Central CRF 009—Japan)
Jimi Hendrix (Eyebic JECD-1030—Japan)
Jimi Hendrix (World Super Hits SH-1709—Japan)
Jimi Hendrix Collection (Graffiti GRCD 12—UK)
Jimi Hendrix Collection (Object OR 0071—UK)
Jimi Hendrix Concerts (Polydor P33P-25038—Japan)
Jimi Hendrix Concerts (Polydor P20P-22014—Japan)
Jimi Hendrix Concerts (Media Motion 1—UK)
Jimi Hendrix Concerts (Warner 22306—US)
Jimi Hendrix Concerts/Radio One (Castle ESBCT 154—UK)
Jimi Hendrix Experience (Signal CD 88110—UK)
Jimi Hendrix Experience (ZETA—France)
Jimi Hendrix—The Interview (CID 006—UK)
Jimi Hendrix/Little Richard—Rock 'n' Roll Special
 (Phono-Music CD926—Germany)
Jimi Hendrix Live (More DV 2041—Italy)
Jimi Hendrix 1970 (Merman/Discussion 1983)
Jimi Hendrix: Auld Lang Syne (JH BG 100-03/04—Italy)
Jimi Hendrix: Inside The Expereince (MediaAmerica)
Jimi Hendrix: Setting The Record Straight (MediaAmerica)
Jimi Hendrix: Volume 1 & 2 (Wisepack LEC 603)
Jimi Hendrix & Traffic: A Session (Oh Boy 9027—Luxembourg)
Jimi Plays Berkeley (BMG 791168—UK)
Jimi Plays Monterey (Warner 25358)
Jimi Plays Monterey (Polydor P20P-22015—Japan)
Jimi Plays Monterey (Polydor P33P-25003—Japan)

Jimi Plays Monterey (Polydor POCP-2026—Japan)
Jimi Plays Monterey (Polydor 827 990—Germany)
Jimi Plays Monterey (Polydor 847 244-2—UK)
Johnny B. Goode (Capitol/EMI 432018-2—Australia)
Kiss The Sky (Reprise 25119-2—USA)
Kiss The Sky (Polydor P20P-22017—Japan)
Kiss The Sky (Polydor P33P-25003—Japan)
Kiss The Sky (Polydor POCP-2029—Japan)
Kiss The Sky (Polydor 823 704—Germany)
The Last Experience (Bescol CD42—Italy)
The Last Experience (Teichiku/Overseas 30CP-232—Japan)
Last American Concert, Vol 1 (TSP 062—Italy)
Last American Concert, Vol 2 (TSP 072—Italy)
The Legendary Star Club Tapes (Early Years 3309)
Lifelines (Reprise 26435—4 CD box set—US)
Live At Cafe Au Go-Go (Koine K880802—Italy)
Live At The Monterey Pop Festival 1967 (Document DR021—Sweden)
Live At Olympia Theater 1/29/68 (Black Panther 017—Italy)
Live At Winterland (Rykodisc RCD 20038—USA)
Live At Winterland (Rykodisc RCD 20038G—USA) gold disc
Live At Winterland +3: The Ultimate Collection (Rykodisc RCD 90038)
Live At Winterland (Polydor P20P-22016—Japan)
Live At Winterland (Polydor P33P-20119—Japan)
Live At Winterland (Polydor POCP-2027—Japan)
Live At Winterland (Polydor 847 238-2—UK)
The Live Collection 1967 (Living Legend LLR 001—Italy)
Live In London 1967 (Koine 881104—Italy)
Live In London 1967 (Black Panther 016—Italy)
Live In Los Angeles Forum 4/26/69 (Black Panther 050—Italy)
Live In New York (Point—Holland)
Live In New York 3/17/68 (Black Panther 018—Italy)
Live In Stockholm (Document 007—Italy)
Live USA (Imtrat 900.036—Germany)
Live & Unreleased The Radio Show (Castle HBCD 100—UK)
Loose Ends (Polydor 837 574-2—Germany)
Loose Ends (Polydor P20P-22011—Japan)
Masterpieces (Pulsar 008—Holland)
The Master's Master (Rockin' JH01)
Message To Love: Randall's Island (Pyramid/Triangle 043—Italy)
Midnight Lightning (Polydor P20P-22013—Japan)
Midnight Lightning (Polydor P33P-25025—Japan)
Midnight Magic (Neutral Zone 89012)
Midnight Shines Down (Blue Kangaroo BK 04—Italy)
Monterey International Pop Festival (Rhino 70596—USA)
Monterey Pop Festival (Document DR 021—Germany)
Monterey Pop Festival (Rhino PRO2-90130—USA)
Monterey Pop Fest, Vol IV (Black Panther 042—Italy)
More Electricity From Newport (Luna LU 9201—Italy)
Musicorama: Paris 1968 (Pyramid/Triangle 043—Italy)
The New York Sessions (Traditional Line 1301—Europe)
Nightlife (Thunderbolt 075—Japan)
Octavia & Univibe (Hal Leonard 00660041) *
Old Gold #1 Collection (Old Gold—UK)
On The Killing Floor (Swinging Pig 012)
The Peel Sessions (Strange Fruit SFPSCD 065—UK)
Prologue (Wild Media 20103 —Japan)
Prologue (Vavan Media HOOW 20103—Japan)
The Psychedelic Voodoo Chile (unknown—UK)
Purple Haze (Success 2101CD-EEC—Holland)
Purple Haze (Polydor 871 459-2—UK)
Purple Haze (On Stage 120010—Italy)
Purple Songs (Lost Rose LR 16—Italy)
Radio Radio (Rykodisc PRO 0078—USA)
Radio One: The BBC Sessions (Rykodisc RCD 20078—USA)
Radio One: The BBC Sessions—pic disc (Rykodisc RCD 20078P—USA)
Radio One (Victor VDP-1454—USA)
Rainbow Bridge (RB 12134—Japan)
Rare Masters Series, Vol 3: Jimi Hendrix (TGP 134—Italy)
Rarities On Compact Disc, Vol 1: Jimi Hendrix (On the Radio 1—USA)
Rarities On Compact Disc, Vol 3: Jimi Hendrix (On the Radio 3—USA)
Record Plant Jam (Pilot HJCD 69—Italy)
Riots In Berkeley (Beech Marten 038)
Rock Legends (Knight RGL 47001—UK)

Rhythm (Hal Leonard 00660043) *
Sessions aka The Studio Box (Polydor 847 232-2—UK 4-CD box set)
Shine On Earth, Shine On (Sidewalk 89010/11—Italy)
Singles Album (Polydor PODVCD 6—UK)
Singles Album (Polydor P58P-20112/3—Japan)
Smash Hits (Polydor 825255—UK)
Smash Hits (Warner 2276—USA)
Smash Hits (Polydor P20P-22003—Japan)
Smash Hits (Polydor P33P-50030—Japan)
Something In The Air, Vol 3 (Old Gold KL03/03—UK sampler)
Spotlight (Sonet SPCD-8—UK)
Stages (Reprise 26732-2—USA)
Stages (Polydor POCP-2161—Japan)
Stages (Warner PRO-CD-5194—USA)
Standing Next To A Mountain (If Six Was Nine JH01—UK)

Star Spangled Blues (Neutral Zone 89011)
Steal This Disc 1 (Rykodisc RCD 00056—USA)
Steal This Disc 2 (Rykodisc RCD 00076—USA)
Steal This Disc 3 (Rykodisc 55328—USA)
Sweet Angel (World Productions 022—Italy)
Things I Used To Do (Early Years 3334—Italy)
The Things I Used To Do (Golden Memories—Italy)
The Ultimate Blues Collection (Castle Comm—France)
The Ultimate Experience (Polydor 517 235-2—UK)
The Wind Cries Mary (Polydor 863 917-2—UK)
UK Rock Heroes (Century CECC 00021—Japan)
Variations On A Theme: Red House (Hal Leonard 00660040)
Voodoo Chile (Galaxis CD 9006—Europe)
War Heroes (Polydor 813 573-2—Germany)
War Heroes (Polydor P20P-22010—Japan)

Wayne's World (Reprise soundtrack—USA)
Whammy Bar & Fingergrease (Hal Leonard 00660038) *
Wild Man Of Pop, Vol 1 (RFT 003—Italy)
Wild Man Of Pop, Vol 2 (RFT 004—Italy)
Winterland Days (Manic Depression 01)
Withnail & I (DRG CDSBL 12590—USA)
Wizard's Visions (World Productions 026—Italy)
Woke Up This Morning & Found Myself Dead
    (Red Lightning 0068—UK)
Woodstock (Mobile Fidelity MFCD 4-816—USA)
Woodstock (Atlantic 500-2—USA)
Woodstock Nation (Wild Bird 890 901/2)
Woodstock Two (Atlantic 400-2—USA)
16 Greatest Classics (Bigtime 261 525-2—Germany)
21 Years Of Alternative Radio 1 (Strange Fruit SFRCD 200—UK)

Compact disc notes:

- *The Last Experience* (Bescol/Overseas) is inappropriately titled. In reality, it is the *Experience* (Bulldog) soundtrack. *Spotlight* (Sonet) and *Jimi Hendrix Experience* (ZETA) also are the same as the *Experience* soundtrack.
- *The Live Collection* (Living Legend) is sometimes catalogued as *Live In Concert 1967*. The material includes two songs from Stockholm, with the remaining 12 tracks taken from the Radio One sessions.
- *Gloria*/Hey Joe/Voodoo Chile/Purple Haze is listed in some catalogues as simply *Jimi Hendrix* (Polydor 887 585-2).
- *The Peel Sessions* (Strange Fruit) is a CD single with five tracks from the Radio One Top Gear sessions.
- The Japanese version of *Radio One* (Victor) contains two additional tracks culled from the *Daytripper* (Rykodisc) CD3.
- *Radio Radio* (Rykodisc) is a five-song radio station sampler of the Radio One sessions.
- *Rock Legends* (Knight) is a sampler of various artists and only contains one Hendrix track—'Red House' from the Scene Club sessions.
- *The Jimi Hendrix Collection* (Graffiti) is an abbreviated version of the 26/4/69 Los Angeles Forum concert released in it's entirety on *Electric Jimi* (Jaguarondi), and included in the *Lifelines* box set.
- The *Old Gold #1 Collection* (Old Gold) is a 10-CD set of various artists with only one Hendrix track—'Voodoo Chile'.
- *21 Years Of Alternative Radio* (Strange Fruit) is a sample of artists from the John Peel produced BBC sessions. The Jimi Hendrix 'Hey Joe' track appears.
- *Crosstown Traffic* is a four-song CD released in conjunction with the use of 'Crosstown Traffic' as music theme bed for European Wrangler Jeans TV commercial. Other tracks are 'Voodoo Chile (Slight Return)', 'All Along The Watchtower' and 'Have You Ever Been (To Electric Ladyland)'.
- *British Beat Live In Germany 1966-67* (Early Years) is a compilation of artists appearing on the Beat Club TV show. The Experience performs 'Hey Joe' and 'Purple Haze.'
- *Daytripper* is a 3' CD released by Rykodisc in conjunction with the *Radio One* release, offering additional bonus tracks. The Japanese release of *Radio One* (Victor) includes these tracks.
- In 1989, Polydor in England released a box set of four compact discs with *Are You Experienced, In The West, Band Of Gypsys* and *War Heroes*.
- *Steal This Disc, Steal This Disc 2, Steal This Disc 3* and *Here It Is—The Music* are samplers of Rykodisc artists. Here It Is was released in a promotion with TDK tapes, and only available in a marketing multi-pack of TDK audio tapes released in 1988.
- *Stages* (Warner PRO-CD-5194) is an 8-song radio station only sampler of the *Stages* four-disc box set.
- *Monterey Pop* (Rhino PRO2-90130) is a 24-track radio station only sampler of various artists from the Monterey box set. It only includes one Experience track—'Killin' Floor'.
- In 1989-90, Reprise re-issued a number of Hendrix releases, 'digitally remastered for superior sonic fidelity.' In the process of doing this, they also changed the tracking on a number of the releases. *Electric Ladyland* was compacted onto a single CD. *Smash Hits* included the additional tracks 'Highway Chile' and '51st Anniversary' from the European release; in addition to the inclusion of CD graphics on the disc. The *Jimi Hendrix Concerts* adds 'Foxy Lady' from the 4/26/69 Los Angeles Forum concert.

- *Fuzz, Feedback* and *Wah Wah, Octavia & Univibe, Rhyth*, and *Whammy Bar & Finger Grease* are a series of educational CDs released as part of the Hal Leonard Reference Series in 1989-90. Each contains 25-40 samples of Hendrix performing the certain effect each piece is named for. These items do no contain complete tracks, but 20-second to three-minute samples taken from various album and concert recordings. Also included in the Hal Leonard series is *Variations On A Theme: Red House*, featuring six complete performances of 'Red House' by Hendrix. The discs were repackaged in 1993 and released with complete transcriptions.
- Pre-Experience material emerged in Japan in 1990 with the release of *Nightlife* (Thunderbolt 075) and *Free Spirit* (Magnum/Thunderbolt 084), containing tracks from the Lonnie Youngblood sessions; and *Prologue* (Wild Media 20103) along with *The Psychedelic Voodoo Child* (Remember 75003), *Experience* (Signal 88110), featuring material from the Curtis Knight period. The repackagings continued as the decade moved on with the Lonnie Youngblood material showing up on *Experiences* (Pulsar 004), *Masterpieces* (Pulsar 008) and *Jimi Hendrix: Volume 1 & 2* (Wisepack) coming out in 1992.
- In 1990, Polydor in England released *Footlights* aka *The Live Box*, and *Sessions* aka *The Studio Box*. Both are 4-CD box sets of previously available Hendrix product. *The Live Box* included: *Live At Winterland; Live At Monterey; Band Of Gypsys*, featuring three additional tracks from the US *Band Of Gypsys 2* release; and *Isle Of Wight*, featuring the soundtrack from the movie. *Sessions* featured digitally remastered versions of Hendrix's four studio albums—*Are You Experienced?, Axis: Bold As Love, Electric Ladyland* and *Cry Of Love.*
- In 1990, Reprise released *Lifelines*, a four-CD box set comprised of the *Live & Unreleased Radio Show* with the addition of the complete 26/4/69 Los Angeles Forum concert.
- The *Are You Experienced?* CD-single (Polydor 879 583-2) released in France in 1991 contains a previously unreleased demo version of 'Come On (Part One)' along with the studio version of 'The Star Spangled Banner' that appeared on the *Rainbow Bridge* album.
- Sampler albums released in 1990 include: *The Ultimate Blues Collection* (Castle Communications), featuring 'Catfish Blues' from the BBC sessions; *Back In Time* (Teledisc), a three-CD set of various artists featuring one Jimi Hendrix Experience track; and *Something In The Air, Vol 3* (Old Gold), a various artists compilation featuring the Experience track 'Hey Joe'.
- *The Best Of & The Rest Of Jimi Hendrix* (Action Replay) contains tracks from the Jim Morrison/Jimi Hendrix Scene Club jam; which has also been released as *The New York Sessions* (Traditional Line) and Woke Up This Morning And Found Myself Dead (Red Lightning). *Jimi Hendrix Experience* (Signal) and *Purple Haze* (Success) contain the same material. Some tracks are from *Woke Up This Morning And Found Myself Dead*, with other tracks from the *Experience* soundtrack. Portions of the Scene Club jam also appear on *Introspective.*
- Interview material of Jimi Hendrix can be found on *Hendrix Speaks* (Rhino 70771), *Introspective* (Tabak CINT 9006), *Jimi Hendrix 1970* (Discussion/Merman 1983) and *Standing Next To A Mountain* (If Six Was Nine). The latter two come in a box set with two additional color photos included.
- Japanese CDs which start with the P33P code were released between 1985 and 1986. Those with P20P were released in 1989. Those with POCP were released in 1991 and are digitally remixed and remastered.

INDEX